Is This Heaven?

Is This Heaven?

The Magic of the Field of Dreams

BRETT H. MANDEL

Guilford, Connecticut

An imprint of The Rowman & Littlefield Publishing Group, Inc.
4501 Forbes Blvd., Ste. 200
Lanham, MD 20706
www.rowman.com

Distributed by NATIONAL BOOK NETWORK

British Library Cataloguing in Publication Information available

Library of Congress Cataloging-in-Publication Data available

ISBN 978-1-4930-5510-4 (paper : alk. paper)
ISBN 978-1-4930-5722-1 (electronic)

♾™ The paper used in this publication meets the minimum requirements of American National Standard for Information Sciences—Permanence of Paper for Printed Library Materials, ANSI/NISO Z39.48-1992.

For Rose Mandel Weinbaum

"Named before thou wert born . . .
My soul prays to God for thee that thou mayest stand in the day of
trial that thy children may be blest of the Lord and thy people,
saved by His power."
—William Penn's Prayer for Philadelphia, 1684

Contents

Acknowledgments

I could not have told this story without a lot of help and support. If I have created anything compelling, it is because so many people shared wonderful stories with me and so many people gave me the assistance I required to make this book a reality. I am pleased to be able to thank the individuals who helped in so many ways to make this book a reality.

I thank my parents, Sharyn Dershowitz and Stephan Mandel, and my entire family for all of their help and encouragement during this publication process. I am lucky to have such loving and supportive relatives. Similarly, I thank my in-laws, the Weinbaums, who have enthusiastically cheered on my efforts.

Thanks are due to *Field of Dreams* veteran David Thornburgh and the staff of the Pennsylvania Economy League, Eastern Division, who lived through the early days of this project. Similarly, I appreciate Philadelphia City Controller Jonathan Saidel, Deputy City Controller Anthony Radwanski, and the staff of the City Controller's Office who allowed me to focus on *Field of Dreams* minutiae when I probably should have been concentrating on municipal finance as this book became a reality.

I must thank John Morris for resurrecting this project and Jill and Jim Langford and Diamond Communications (and Rowman & Littlefield

Publishing Group) for all of their moral support, faith, and hard work to make the manuscript ready for publication.

I am grateful for assistance from many sources during the research and writing of this book. While I know that in creating any list, I risk omitting some people who were helpful, I must single out a few people who were particularly helpful to me in my work or genuinely selfless with their time and assistance.

Special appreciation is reserved for Al and Rita Ameskamp, Betty Boeckenstedt, and Don and Becky Lansing. Their warm reception, good cheer, and hospitality made my visits to Dyersville very special. Wendol Jarvis, Keith and Jacque Rahe, and Eldon Trumm were similarly generous with their time and information.

I am especially indebted to Jim Bohn, Jerry and Lynn Ryan, Minister Terry Rush, Christopher Albrecht and Mark Babiarz, and Kent and John Nelson, who were all so honest and open with their accounts of their experiences with the Field of Dreams. Their tales are more than illustrative for my purposes; they are genuinely moving. I hope I was able to capture in my narrative what made their stories so intriguing.

Tim Crescenti, a consistent supporter of this project, has provided invaluable information, inspiration, and counsel. Bill Rediger of the Dyersville Commercial allowed me to dig through archival photographs and articles and was wonderfully hospitable on a cold Dyersville day. Karla Thompson provided much-needed background on her part of the world.

Sungman Cho, Hiraki Tanaka, and Mineko Frost aided with some translations from Japanese into English. Elliot Weinbaum helped track down many esoteric texts and articles, John DiTullio helped wade through piles of old newspaper and magazine articles, and Nicole Mandel and David Kelliher assembled critical video information. National Baseball Hall of Fame and Museum librarian James Gates Jr. was extremely generous with his time and assistance digging up baseball-specific information. Joe Scherrman provided me with an entertaining and informative video of the Ghost Players' trip to Japan. Additionally,

I extend my thanks to Mountain Lion, Inc., for helping to develop this work and shape the treatment in its formative stages.

Finally, and most significantly, I thank the person to whom I owe more than I can possibly acknowledge. My wife, Laura Weinbaum, fixes all that is wrong with a smile and brightens every day with her presence. She listens to stories she cannot possibly find interesting, laughs at me when I take myself too seriously, and makes me deliriously happy in every way. For this book project, she cheerfully rode shotgun on a trip to Dyersville, allowed me to fixate on my writing when I should have been paying attention to her, and edited the messy pages of early drafts, adding needed polish. Her touch is evident on every page of the book. If I started today and worked constantly for the next thousand years, I could never adequately express to her how thankful I am to have her in my life.

Foreword

In the thirty-one years since we shot *Field of Dreams* on Don Lansing's farm, not much has changed there. Sure, there are little details that are different, but it's still as beautiful and peaceful as when we first drove down that long driveway, across Hewitt Creek, to arrive at the beautiful green gem of a baseball field surrounded by corn.

But the truth is a little more complicated than the field's simple beauty. Only the most diehard fans of the film know that the beautiful ball field was actually built across two farmers' properties. The filmmakers' choice to place it there began something of a feud between Lansing and his neighbors, Al and Rita Ameskamp, that made national news.

Terrence Mann predicted in the film, "People will come." Indeed they did, by the hundreds of thousands. And although the movie fades out as an endless line of cars are pulling into the driveway, the film offers no advice as to how the farmers were supposed to deal with the sudden onslaught of humanity.

But for all of the logistical problems the field's popularity has caused, I have always thought it touching that neither farmer ever charged an admission fee to the movie site. How easy it would have been to ask for a dollar or five and how quickly people would have given it ("for it is money they have, and peace they lack"), but they never asked.

Where else can so many people wander such a beautifully maintained, privately owned park for free?

I have been back to the field maybe twenty times in the intervening years and I experience a bit of the *Field of Dreams* magic every time I visit, even once in the dead of winter. Of course, there was the "celebrity" game where I got to bat against the great Bob Gibson and another where I sang karaoke with Hall-of-Famer Wade Boggs and especially at the twenty-fifth anniversary celebration when Kevin and I reenacted our game of catch for Bob Costas and a few thousand fans before we watched the movie on the same field we shot it on—all incredible experiences.

But the trips to the field I remember most fondly were the ones when there weren't crowds and celebrities; just regular folks wandering around the field, walking into the corn and "having a catch" on the infield. Once I was invited to play in a pickup game of LDS ministers, who had made the half-hour drive to the movie site from their convention in Dubuque. We had a great time goofing around on the field for almost an hour before they recognized me as having been in the movie.

Beyond explaining the fascinating history of the field and the circumstances that caused it to be chosen out of the thousands of other similar farms in the Midwest, what Brett Mandel captures so well in this book is the overwhelming emotional impact the movie and, by extension, the field have had on so many people's lives.

When I am recognized by fans in public as having played John Kinsella, I am frequently told how often they watch the movie for inspiration (or a good cry), and then I am sometimes told tearful memories of their own father's dedication to (or abandonment of) them. Both can bring tears and I find myself hugging and crying with a stranger in an airport or grocery store over our lost fathers. (My own father, Walter, died unexpectedly thirty-six days before I shot the famous final scene in 1988).

It has become clear that *Field of Dreams* has miraculously risen to be considered the iconic movie of our generation, despite being called by *Rolling Stone* magazine at the time, "the worst movie of 1989." It has been enshrined in the National Film Registry of the Library of Congress and has inspired MLB to play a major league game this year at the movie site. Lines and images from the film ("If you build it . . . he will come", "Is this Heaven?", "Wanna have a catch?") have become part of our national lexicon and have been used to sell everything from insurance to Eternal Life.

For anyone who has ever enjoyed the movie and wanted to know more about it, or even those who have been confounded by its popularity, I encourage you to sit back and enjoy Brett's wonderful, true tale of a magical movie that has left so many of us simultaneously smiling and in tears, and wondering to ourselves, "Is this Heaven?"

—Dwier Brown, actor and author of
*If You Build It . . . : A Book about
Fathers, Fate and Field of Dreams*

Introduction

I never really planned to write a book about the *Field of Dreams* movie site. I liked the film *Field of Dreams* and, like many, cried at the ending. But I like a lot of films, and I am an easy mark for a weepy movie. Nothing about the film or my fondness for it would have suggested that, some day, I would write about *Field of Dreams* and how it has inspired a pilgrimage to the still-surviving movie site.

But, much as Ray Kinsella heard that voice in film, I had a calling. For me, it was nothing mystical. The voice that came to me was the voice of an agent on the phone. Ray Kinsella heard, "If you build it, he will come." I heard a less ethereal offer to explore the idea of a book about the *Field of Dreams* movie site near Dyersville, Iowa, and how it had become a pop culture mecca. That was 1996.

I liked the idea and began my exploration of the phenomena surrounding Dyersville's unique attraction. I worked for a number of months conducting research, creating a book proposal, and putting together some writing. In essence, I suggested that my book would try to explain why people from all over the world were traveling to Dyersville to visit a former movie set and why they were not just going there to take pictures but were visiting in search of a setting for some deeply personal emotional experiences.

We pitched the idea and received some positive responses, but no publisher offered to fund the project. Just as Ray Kinsella spent many nights looking at the field he created waiting for something to happen, I dashed to the mailbox and jumped when the phone rang, hoping I would receive good news about the book proposal. "Shoeless" Joe Jackson appeared for Ray, but I received no positive news. So the *Field of Dreams* book files were packed away, and I moved on to other projects. I thought a lot about Dyersville's attraction but considered the matter closed.

In 2000, like a voice from out of the corn, a fellow author called and asked whether I would share the idea for the book about the *Field of Dreams* with his publisher. Suddenly, the project was moving forward again.

I did much of my research for the project over the phone and in libraries in 1996. In 2000, I was able to find a wealth of information by using the Internet. But, of course, the only way to truly explore whether there is magic in the Dyersville corn was to hit the road. More than three years after I had decided I would never get a chance to tell the story, I found myself standing on the Field of Dreams, laughing at myself for the silly grin I sported, feeling as if I had stepped through the looking glass and into something uniquely charmed.

I have been fortunate enough in my life to have visited significant sites across the globe and have walked in famous footsteps of biblical figures and historical luminaries. I have stood on ground considered holy and have pondered events that changed the world within the walls where they occurred.

I cannot say that my visit to the Field of Dreams could generate the same chills I felt watching the pious in Rome or Jerusalem or thinking about the tremendous events that transpired in Independence Hall or at Gettysburg.

That said, there was something very special about standing on the Field of Dreams. It did not take much imagination at all to believe that I was not just at the place where *Field of Dreams* was filmed, but I was actually part of an ongoing story that simply included the chapter told by Hollywood.

I spent my time in Dyersville throwing batting practice, swinging for the corn, meeting visitors, and talking to people whose lives had been changed by the field. During my months of research, I consulted scholarly tomes and entertainment magazines. I viewed *Field of Dreams* and watched videos about people who traveled to Dyersville. I spoke to movie stars and major leaguers and interviewed dozens of people for whom the Field of Dreams is much more than just a tourist attraction.

Putting the book together was both fun and moving. I nearly took the head off a little leaguer when I lined his batting practice pitch back up the middle. I grooved a fat pitch to a middle-aged man who hit one into the corn and then whooped around the bases in triumph. I wiped tears from my eyes as I ran up my long-distance bills listening to people describe what the Field of Dreams meant to them.

I had a great time in Dyersville and really enjoyed learning some of the behind-the-scenes stories about the filming of *Field of Dreams* and the goings-on at the Field of Dreams. I was touched by the people who opened up to me and shared some very personal stories. A few had to pause to keep from choking up while talking. Some cried as they spoke.

The tale of the continuing pilgrimage to the Field of Dreams is more than just a tale of camera-toting tourists or souvenir-seeking movie buffs. It is the tale of people who seek something significant in a world that often denies the spiritual, of people who seek ways to communicate powerful emotions, and of people who visit a baseball field, not for batting practice but for redemption.

I am really glad that I had a chance to tell this story.

The Story of the Field of Dreams

"If you build it, he will come."

—*The Voice*

The film *Field of Dreams* debuted in Dubuque, Iowa, in April 1989. Just three months later, twelve-year-old Matt Bohn died in the crash of United Airlines Flight 232 across the state in Sioux City. Matt's flight crashed into an anonymous Iowa cornfield, but a very special Iowa cornfield would help his family cope with the tragedy, just as it would touch the lives of countless others. Built to bring a work of fiction to life as a film, the Field of Dreams just outside Dyersville, Iowa, has been transformed from a movie set into a pop culture mecca and secular hallowed ground.

When Matt boarded his plane, nobody—not his family, not the *Field of Dreams* filmmakers, not the owners of the Field of Dreams site—knew what the future would bring. The little leaguer had been on his way from Denver to Pittsburgh to return home to his parents after visiting family in Colorado. Shortly into the flight, an engine exploded, and flying shrapnel severed all three of the jet's hydraulic lines. The pilots were left with little control over their aircraft. In dire peril, the pilots used engine thrust from the jet's remaining engines to steady the flight and prepared for an emergency landing at the Sioux Gateway Airport.

Emergency personnel assembled to meet the imperiled flight. The hundreds who gathered prepared for the worst and held their collective breath as Flight 232 began its descent. For a moment, it seemed as if the crippled jet would land safely, but its right wing tip touched down first, causing the aircraft to burst into flames, cartwheel off the runway, and break into three pieces.

Somehow, 184 travelers survived. Matt and his grandmother, Lena Blaha, who was traveling with him, were among the 112 who perished in the fiery disaster.

Back in western Pennsylvania, Matt's father Jim, mother Cindy, and sister Stephanie drove to the airport to meet the flight, unaware of the drama that was unfolding in the Midwest. Arriving at the Pittsburgh airport, the Bohns saw a local television news van and learned that a plane was down in Iowa. They had no reason to be concerned until they noticed that Matt's flight was not listed on the monitor that tracked arrivals.

While Matt's family quickly discovered that it was Matt's flight that had crashed, they were unable to learn whether Matt and his grandmother were on board or whether they had been harmed. The Bohns had to return home unsure whether Matt and Lena had survived and wondering how the coming news could alter their lives.

Hours of frantic calls, anxious wondering, and prayer brought no answers. A Sioux City hospital reported that a boy who fit Matt's description was being treated in one of its wards, but positive identification was not yet possible. Jim Bohn was desperate for news. Finally, the airline agreed to fly him to Iowa, but because he could not find a convenient flight, he accepted a ride on a charter flight from the same local television station that first told him of the crash. He left unsure of whether he was going to Iowa to help care for Matt or take on the grim duty of claiming his remains.

Jim was a high school physical education teacher who served as a coach for his son—a blossoming second baseman—on the baseball diamond. He was used to young people counting on him for guidance and looking to him as a role model. He left his home, hoping his son could count on him that day.

When he arrived in Iowa, Jim went from hospital to hospital, trying to find his son among the survivors, but Matt was not among any of the recovering passengers. Jim knew the awful truth. Matt was the first of the victims to be identified and was released to his father.

Jim's visit to Iowa lasted just three days and two nights, but it changed his life forever. He was shattered. But amid the tragic circumstances surrounding his visit, Jim found a bit of solace. Just weeks before, the Bohn family celebrated Matt's birthday by going to see *Field of Dreams*. The film's tale of the power of dreams and a special Iowa cornfield brought the family together.

At their home, Cindy and Stephanie Bohn sat in Matt's room staring at the ticket stub from the family's night at the movie, freshly recovered from Cindy's purse. The ticket for *Field of Dreams* was dated May 7, 1989. It had been Matt's twelfth and last birthday.

In Iowa, Jim was housed in a college dormitory where he spent much of his time staring out his window, thinking about the past—and the future. Amid his family's suffering, Jim had an inspiration: "When I was out in Iowa and I looked out the dorm room window and saw a baseball field bordered by a cornfield, it just all hit me."

He had previously associated the film *Field of Dreams* with the relationship between himself and his father. Now he saw a connection between himself and his own son. "We saw the movie on Matt's birthday," he said. "And when the movie was over, I remember saying to Cindy that there was a message there for me, but I didn't know what it was. But I knew it was telling me something, and I thought it was telling me a message about me and my dad. I didn't know it was about me and my son."

At home in western Pennsylvania late that summer, Jim read in a local paper that the *Field of Dreams* movie set could be found near Dyersville, Iowa, and that—just like in the film—people were coming to visit it. Jim sat down to write a difficult letter asking an Iowa farmer whose land had been the setting for the film to keep the attraction intact for an additional season so that the Bohns could visit it on the anniversary of Matt's death:

> You don't know me; my name is Jim Bohn. My son Matt and mother-in-law Lena Blaha died in the crash of United Airlines Flight 232 in Sioux City on July 19.
>
> This past spring I had taken my son and family to see the movie "Field of Dreams." We loved the movie. I had no idea that the "field" was still there. I figured that after the filming it had been replanted. To my surprise and delight, I read an article last evening in our Pittsburgh (PA.) Press newspaper that you have been maintaining the field. How long do you plan to maintain it as the baseball field? Will you still receive visitors next summer? We are planning to visit Sioux City next summer for the anniversary of the crash and would love to stop and visit the field.
>
> Matt was 12 and loved baseball. So do I, as my father before me did. I've always coached Matt's team. For the past 6 years we have had a great time enjoying each other and baseball.
>
> As you may know the plane crashed in an Iowa corn field. I found the whole idea very ironic; the story of an Iowa corn farmer who plows up his corn field to make a baseball field where dreams come true and my son, who loved baseball, dying in an Iowa corn field. My dreams came to an end.
>
> When I was in Sioux City after the crash, I stayed at Briar Cliff College. From my room the most prominent object in the landscape was a baseball field. I could not stop thinking about the movie, the crash and a corn field in Iowa. There was message there.
>
> When I read the article last evening I knew I had to visit the "field." Please let me know of your plans for the field. I hope I will have the chance to walk with my son one more time.

Jim said the letter was basically a question "Can I come? Kind of like in the movie when they ask if they can play." He followed up his letter with a phone call to the man whose farm had served as a movie set and had suddenly turned into an unlikely tourist attraction. Bohn remembered asking whether the field would remain intact. The response was simply that it would remain as is "as long as people came."

The next July, Jim, Cindy, and Stephanie Bohn set off on a drive—the idea of flying made them uneasy—from western Pennsylvania to Colorado to see the family Matt had been visiting with when he took his fateful flight. Along the way, the Bohns stopped at the Field of Dreams—now transformed into something much more meaningful than a movie set. The visit coincided with Jim's birthday, just days before the one-year anniversary of Matt's death. Even though the journey could not bring Matt back, the field could bring his family a measure of comfort.

"At first, it was so soon after my son's death," Matt's father said. "I don't know if I was really thinking anything, and then as the time came, I'm thinking, 'Well, he died in Iowa; the last time I talked to him was on my birthday when he called from my sister-in-law's. I want to go here to feel close to him.' Not so much close to him—all I had to do is go in his bedroom and I felt close to him. But he'll be here. I had a feeling that maybe he would be there—in spirit."

Jim not only came to the field looking to take away a sense of connection with his son but also brought with him a few tokens that he wanted to leave behind. He placed a bat that he and Matt had played with, balls they used for playing catch, and one of Matt's baseball gloves amid the corn surrounding the Field of Dreams. The gesture was a show of fatherly love, a sacrifice to the higher powers that watch over baseball players everywhere, and a way to form a bond with something that had resonated with him.

Jim, a soft-spoken, thoughtful man, described the visit as "comforting, healing, rewarding." But for a man who lost his son, one of the most important aspects of the trip was the ability to somehow reconnect to that which he had lost.

"I always find connections with things, and people tell me, 'You're just imagining that' or 'You're making more out of something than it is,'" Jim said. "And I said, 'Maybe. But, maybe I'm just attuned to it and I see it. There's always connections there, but unless you're attuned to it, you don't see it.'"

Jim and Cindy had joined a bereavement group called Compassionate Friends for parents whose children had died young. The group's symbol was a butterfly, emblematic of the metamorphosis of a young spirit shuffling off its mortal shell to move on after death. Since joining the group, Jim associated his son with the butterfly and always thought of Matt when he saw one. At the Field of Dreams, Jim, Cindy, and Stephanie posed for pictures with the Iowa farmer whose land hosted most of the Field of Dreams. As they posed, they noticed a butterfly making lazy loops around the group. Perhaps it was just a butterfly and nothing more, but for a grieving family it was a comforting to think that a part of Matt could still be with them.

Walking away from the Field of Dreams, Jim Bohn realized that the trip accomplished more than he had hoped. At first, he confessed, his hopes had been elevated. "I wanted to see Matt come walking out of the cornfield," he confessed. "And then I said, 'Jim, that's not what's going to happen here.' I just kind of had to wake myself up."

But the trip helped him not only come to terms with his loss but also find a way to move forward. "I think it was good in that it—even though I was going out there for whatever was going to be in relation to Matt, it drew my daughter and me closer," he reflected. "I just remember coming away having had a sense of Matt while there but that I left having done things with Stephanie there . . . that helped a bonding."

Using words customarily reserved for religious shrines or sacred places, Jim Bohn spoke of his experience at the Field of Dreams. "I didn't get that real, deep, emotional feeling," he said. "But I did come away in peace."

The tale of how Jim, Cindy, and Stephanie Bohn turned to a stage for make-believe to help them weather the storm of an all-too-real calamity is a remarkable story. "It's a fictional place that has become a real place," Jim said. But the Bohns' story, and tales like it, have become almost commonplace at the Field of Dreams. For more than a decade

now, men, women, and children have come to the tiny town of Dyersville to visit a movie set and experience the magic they believe can be
found within the chalk lines of the Field of Dreams. Once-productive
Iowa farmland turned into a movie set and then evolved as a very special destination.

Make-believe places are able to establish a tug at people's hearts and
minds—some kitschy, some spiritual, but all quite real despite the contrived nature of the actual sites. The acreage that served as the setting
for Kevin Costner's and Ray Liotta's quest for redemption and fulfillment through the mystical elements of America's national pastime has
become a destination for people searching for something. People from
across the globe have found their way to this diamond to race around
the bases, shag fly balls, knock one out of the park, and connect with
something missing in their lives.

The people of Dyersville cannot say they weren't warned. *Field of
Dreams* foretold the pilgrimage that began just weeks after the film
debuted and has continued to today.

"People will come," predicted the character Terence Mann in *Field
of Dreams*. More than ten years after Hollywood transformed the fields
of two Dyersville farmers into a baseball diamond, people have turned
off a narrow country road, down one of a pair of short gravel drives,
and onto the farms of Don Lansing and Al and Rita Ameskamp—more
than fifty thousand visitors each year, perhaps as many as one million
visitors to date, and counting.

Field of Dreams may center around fictional farmer Ray Kinsella's
ability to conjure a connection with his late father—and "Shoeless" Joe
Jackson—out of the Iowa corn, but the tangible remains of the story's
magic have come to mean much more to its visitors. People have come
to Dyersville and the Field of Dreams for a variety of reasons and have
walked away with an astounding array of moving experiences. Fathers
and sons have cemented tattered relationships with a game of catch on
the magical field. Families have found relief from stress and a sanctuary
away from their hectic everyday lives just wandering along the foul lines.

This book is an account of a remnant from an author's and filmmaker's imagination, transformed into a shrine and sanctified by the faithful who have something special on a grass and dirt movie set. Most of all, this book is the story of how a small corner of picturesque farmland has been transformed from a rich patch of earth that produced a lucrative cash crop into a place that produces profound changes in its visitors—changes that have been as nourishing as the most succulent Iowa corn.

A UNIQUE ATTRACTION

The term *redemption* never appears in a baseball box score, and the word *reconciliation* is usually left out of most sportscasters' descriptions of last night's ball game. While a sacrifice can be an integral part of a big inning, baseball does not often have much to do with a shrine, a pilgrimage, or heaven. But at the Field of Dreams, redemption and reconciliation are noted more carefully than strikes or balls, and talk of a shrine, a pilgrimage, and even heaven drowns out talk of runs, hits, or errors. In a small town at the heart of America, on a baseball field carved into a cornfield, these words describe the experiences of visitors who search for something they need in their lives and find peace in an extraordinary location.

When the Dyersville farms of Don Lansing and Al and Rita Ameskamp were turned into a movie set for the filming *of Field of Dreams,* there was no way to tell that it would bring more than Kevin Costner and James Earl Jones to town. But the film's story about ghosts and dreams—too fanciful for many reviewers to take seriously—resonated with those who suspended their disbelief. Looking to discover whether second chances could actually be found in the Dyersville corn and whether heaven is indeed nestled on an Iowa farm, a trickle of visitors began to journey to the former movie set in 1989. Buoyed by remarkable stories recounted by those who made the trip, the Field of Dreams grew from a temporary Hollywood back lot to a destination for tens of thousands of visitors each year. It is not unusual for thousands of people to visit the field on a peak weekend.

The field's tenders have become unlikely soothsayers for their tribe of visitors, working an enchantment as benevolent hosts. In an attempt to capture its magic, the Carolina Mudcats of the Double A Southern League flew Don Lansing to Zebulon, North Carolina, where he sprinkled a bucket full of dirt from the Field of Dreams onto the infield of new Five County Stadium to inaugurate the park in 1991. The Mudcats had a lackluster run from 1966 to 1976, but Lansing's dirt may have been magical for some 1991 Mudcats players—pitcher Tim Wakefield and first baseman Kevin Young carried a little Field of Dreams dirt on their spikes all the way to the majors.

Al and Rita Ameskamp made vials of Field of Dreams dirt available for anyone who wanted to make a small donation. The Ameskamps, tickled by their newfound celebrity, laughed about being asked to autograph ears of corn but wouldn't hazard a guess as to how many vials of "Dream Dirt" have been purchased over the years. They proudly recalled sessions when they used a five-gallon bucket of dirt to prepare hundreds of vials at a time.

The plastic containers of Iowa soil (now decorated with a tasteful "Dream Dirt" logo and an affidavit of authenticity that reads, "This certifies that Dream Dirt is from the original left & center Field of Dreams, Dyersville, Iowa") may be one of the most popular souvenirs for visitors. One man even ordered hundreds of vials and gave them out as favors at his wedding.

In one of his columns, *Chicago Sun-Times* travel writer Bob Puhala sheepishly admitted to taking home one such vial. When confronted by his wife about his buying dirt, he responded, "It's not just dirt. It's . . . well, kind of hard to explain." Puhala's wife reluctantly accepted the dirt and the explanation that it represented all the memories of all the hours her husband played ball throughout his life. Still, she demanded, "Just put the dirt in the drawer when company comes over."

The Ameskamps were not the only ones to promote a unique gift. After renovating their home's picket fence, the Lansings took the pickets from the fence that appeared in the film *Field of Dreams*, cleaned them up, added a note to vouch for their authenticity, and offered them to souvenir seekers. Dozens of visitors brought home pickets from the Field of Dreams along with memories of their trip to Iowa.

Although some of the people of Dyersville have been irritated by the influx of outsiders and their seemingly odd quest for something mystical in the usually quiet corner of the world—and some have even expressed petty jealousies over the perception that their neighbors have undeservedly cashed in on the lucky break that Hollywood chose their land as a movie set—most seem to have enthusiastically embraced the presence of the field and its resulting economic impact. They don't quite know what to make of the nearly ceaseless parade of tourists, but as the crowds have come and gone, the townsfolk have largely respond to the influx of international visitors with pleasant bewilderment and even costumed involvement in the fantasy.

In the summer of 1990, local farmer Keith Rahe organized a team of Ghost Players to entertain Field of Dreams visitors and re-create the image of old-time players emerging from the corn to frolic once again on the enchanted baseball diamond. The Ghost Players—fully clad in authentic 1919 Chicago White Sox uniforms—now include a veterinarian, a state representative, a college baseball coach, and several players who appeared in the film *Field of Dreams* as ballplayers. Frequently asked for autographs, these neighbors have become popular entertainers, traveling the world to spread a little magic from the corn.

LIGHTS, CAMERA, ACTION

The 1989 film *Field of Dreams*, written and directed by Phil Alden Robinson, is based on the 1982 book *Shoeless Joe* by William Patrick (W. P.) Kinsella. Both the film and the book revolve around the power of dreams and the magic of second chances. In the film, child-of-the-sixties-turned-middle-aged-Iowa-farmer Ray Kinsella is able to establish a bond with his late father through a journey that begins with the seemingly irrational action of transforming his rows of corn into a baseball field—and ends with an acceptance that the magic created by that baseball field is not only rational but real. By creating his magical baseball field, farmer Kinsella earns his chance at redemption, and by using the field to say what he could not say, he wins his reconciliation.

Field of Dreams debuted in 1989, promoted with the tag line, "If you believe the impossible, the incredible can come true." The film tells the incredible tale of Iowa farmer Ray Kinsella, who hears a mysterious voice declare, "If you build it, he will come," and plows under a portion of his cornfield to build a baseball diamond. The action, seen as lunacy by his neighbors but supported by his family, succeeds in conjuring the ghost of "Shoeless" Joe Jackson (his father's hero) on the outfield grass of the spectral field. An extraordinary outfielder, Jackson became a baseball pariah after being banned from the game for his involvement in the "Black Sox" scandal, in which eight members of the Chicago White Sox conspired to accept bribes to throw the 1919 World Series. However, thanks to Kinsella's field, which seems to be a portal to an afterlife, Jackson and the other disgraced White Sox players are able once again to play ball.

But the voice has more demands of Kinsella. Despite the fact that he faces losing his farm due to increasing debt, Kinsella travels across the country to obey his interpretations of the voice's commands. He first journeys to Boston where he picks up celebrated but reclusive writer Terence Mann. Mann accompanies Kinsella on his journey—grudgingly at first but soon enthusiastically as he, too, becomes swept up in the magic.

Both Kinsella and Mann face psychological challenges. The Iowa farmer who created the magical ballfield carries guilt because he was unable to repair his damaged relationship with his deceased father. The writer who refuses to publish new stories despite his fans' pleas is scarred by memories of the demolition of Ebbets Field and the Brooklyn Dodgers' move to Los Angeles. Unified by their distinct longings despite their odd-couple appearance, the unlikely pair continues the trek to Minnesota.

In the Land of 10,000 Lakes, Kinsella slips through a window in time and encounters Archibald "Moonlight" Graham, who played one inning in the major leagues in 1905 before retiring from the game to become a doctor. Graham, who never realized his dream of stepping up to the plate for a big league at-bat, is happy to have made such a significant contribution as a doctor, but he still wonders about what could have been. Kinsella, Mann, and a young version of Archie Graham return to Iowa to await the next magical development.

In Iowa, Mann finally experiences the fantasy of ghost baseball, and Graham finally fulfills his dream of having a major league at-bat. But Kinsella and his wife Annie must deal with the real-life threat of losing their farm and its special field to Annie's brother, Mark, who is threatening to foreclose on the property's mortgage. Kinsella's young daughter, Karin, believes she sees a way out of the financial trouble and predicts that the magical baseball field would attract paying customers who would be the salvation of the farm. Mann expands on the vision declaring that people would journey to the enchanted field and save the farm by gladly paying to enjoy the ghostly game of baseball and the memories it would recall.

The film reaches a climax when Karin is knocked to the ground during ongoing arguments between Kinsella and his brother-in-law. A lifeless Karin is revived by Archie Graham, who steps off the magic field and is transformed into an older version of himself—Doctor Graham. The older, wiser Graham concludes that it was not a true tragedy that he never fulfilled his baseball dream, but it would have been a tragedy if he had never become a doctor.

Mann's pain is eased when he is invited to follow the ghost players into the corn and whatever waits beyond. Not only does this unique experience help him come to terms with the game of baseball and his feelings that the game betrayed him; it urges him on to reconnect with those who were inspired by his stories as he vows to write again.

Finally, it is Ray Kinsella's turn. The story of the power of faith, the joy of redemption, and the ability of baseball to link the generations now liberates its protagonist. Ray is left alone on the field with a young catcher—his father incarnated as the young ballplayer he was years before Ray was born. As dusk falls on the field, Ray and his father talk and find reconciliation. As grown-men viewers reach for the tissues to dab watery eyes, Ray seals his redemption by asking, "Hey, Dad, you wanna have a catch?" The film ends with Ray and his father throwing a ball back and forth on the special field. The first carloads of visitors ready to pay to see the game begin to pull up the dirt road followed by a line of cars that stretches to the horizon. The field will be saved as the prophecy is realized, and the pilgrimage starts as the credits roll.

THE FARM TOY CAPITAL OF THE WORLD

When W. P. Kinsella wrote *Shoeless Joe*, he did not realize that a true Field of Dreams could have some of the power of his literary creation. Given its imaginative premises and vivid imagery, it is not surprising that one of Kinsella's books inspired a film. But not only did *Shoeless Joe* inspire a film; it inspired a unique event that has gone beyond life imitating art. When Kevin Costner, James Earl Jones, and Ray Liotta wrapped up their filming duties, they had no notion that their portrayals would encourage thousands of others to repeat their journey of redemption to Iowa.

Before filmmakers found tiny Dyersville, Iowa, the community had enjoyed a mostly quiet existence. Just twenty-five miles west of Dubuque, about a five-hour drive from Chicago, the now predominately German American town was founded in 1848 by an English store owner named James Dyer who left his homeland for America to make his fortune. Dyer purchased land from the U.S. government and, with a handful of other families, made his home on the rich eastern Iowa soil. Ernest Hemingway's ancestors were among those who followed the same path from England to settle in Dyersville.

As the home to three prominent toy manufacturers and the National Farm Toy Museum, Dyersville had been most renowned as the "Farm Toy Capital of the World." In fact, with its numerous stores along its main thoroughfares hawking tiny tractors, miniature cars, and model trucks, Dyersville seems more suited to be associated with the film *Toy Story* than *Field of Dreams*. In the past, visitors came to the unique Becker Woodcarving Museum and its collection of the work of Iowa woodcarver Jack Becker or to the Dyer/Botsford Doll Museum, housed in the grand and ornate Victorian-era Queen Anne home of Dyersville's founder. People seeking salvation or inspiration in Dyersville came to the twin-spired Basilica of St. Francis Xavier—a rare basilica in a rural setting—to sit in its carved wooden pews or marvel at its stained glass windows and gothic architecture, charmingly out of place in the Midwest. But that would all change when Hollywood came calling.

Just a few miles outside the town, where 3,800 people nestle along the meandering Maquoketa River, the Lansing and Ameskamp farms emerge from the gently rolling flatness of the American prairie. But amid the fields, where the rich earth yields eight-foot stalks of corn, a tiny baseball field looks somehow perfectly natural.

Dyersville is not quite quaint, but it is friendly and functional, a town where people meet each other with warm greetings and take note of strangers with cordial hellos. The Dyersville Area Chamber of Commerce describes the region as "a real place in the land mistaken for heaven in the classic movie *Field of Dreams*; a place where traditional values and easy smiles have not gone out of style; a place where dreams come true."

In Dyersville, "Who were you before?" means "What is your maiden name?" and people say "Katie bar the door" when trouble brews. Residents referring to a farm, home, or tractor are sure to mention its previous owners even if they are long gone— "Yes, I live on the old Johnson farm." Visitors asking directions to "the field" receive explicit instructions and no quizzical looks, but anyone asking for "the toy factory" will be asked, "Which one?"

Like all small communities, Dyersville struggles to maintain employment and provide family-sustaining work that can enable it to retain residents and maintain the viability of the town. This need is especially acute in Iowa, which has lost population in recent decades, especially during the 1980s farm crisis that threatened the survival of the state's many family farms. The Hawkeye State still struggles to retain young people after they graduate from high school. But with manufacturing, tourism, and agriculture providing a diverse employment base, Dyersville is more viable than many neighboring towns.

By day, the town is largely empty as residents leave for work. At night, backlit fluorescent signs hawk fast food and motel rooms for rent just off the highway. In town, cobra lights brighten the empty main street, and the glowing spires of the basilica shine placidly in the sky. Lights from Dyersville Community Park ballfields glow late in the evening to illuminate baseball and softball games for participants of all ages.

If it is possible to summarize the essence of a town on a police patch, Dyersville's finest attempted it by placing the basilica across an unfurled U.S. flag and adding a baseball field, a farm tractor, a representation of the Heritage Trail—a nature pathway that stretches from Dyersville to Dubuque—and a few lush trees. That is Dyersville.

Checkerboarded by wide, shaded avenues running east to west cut perpendicularly by broad, tree-lined streets running north to south, the 4.5-square miles of Dyersville are divided neatly into unequal quadrants by 1st Street and 1st Avenue. With all streets in town numbered, directions are fairly simple—turn left at 3rd Street and go two blocks, or go right at 2nd Avenue and travel three blocks—but, because all streets are wide enough to allow a quick U-turn, anyone who did not realize that 3rd Street followed 2nd Street could immediately reverse course.

Traveling east through Dyersville on 1st Avenue, one finds the stately basilica dominates the northwest quadrant, its spires rising more than two hundred feet over the two-story town. Across the 1st Avenue Bridge, turn-of-the-century buildings housing the town bank and the local newspaper are interspersed with more modern, nondescript professional offices and practical stores along the town's main street.

Further east, the 1929 Memorial Building houses city hall and the public library across from the former home of Dyersville's founder.

Winding north along 6th Street and then east along 2nd Avenue, visitors find Route 136 traveling north past train tracks where the Illinois Central passes through town. Just beyond, a decommissioned army tank marks the trail head where the Heritage Trail begins its journey, stretching east through picturesque bluffs and meandering streams to Dubuque along the old Chicago Great Western Railway. Nearby, the large, blue water tower emblazoned with "Dyersville" rises above the trees over the playing fields and recreational areas of Dyersville Commercial Club Park.

Following Route 136 a short distance north, the first sign directs visitors toward the *Field of Dreams* movie site along Dyersville East Road. Just outside the town limits and about three miles along the winding road, past a cluster of anonymous suburban ranch homes and the seemingly endless rolling hills of corn, Lansing Road leads down a short drive to a pair of short gravel roads into the corn—and the Field of Dreams.

The spindly light poles first call attention to the presence of something out of the ordinary among the farm houses and fields of growing crops. To say the field looks as it did in the film does not do the scene justice. Instead, it appears to visitors as if they had arrived at Ray Kinsella's magical field the day after the film's climactic moment. The carloads of visitors seem to be part of the endless caravan that was glimpsed before the credits rolled. One would not be surprised to see Ray, Annie, and Karin sitting on the porch swing.

With cars stowed on a simple gravel lot, the spectacle can be seen in all its simple majesty—manicured green grass and red-brown dirt embellished by a small fenced backstop and tiny wooden grandstands. An American flag on a short pole stirs in right field with lazy breezes that carry the scent of manure through the surrounding corn and across the land. With the classic white farmhouse and red barn overlooking the scene, visitors old and young take their places at the site like an omnipresent cast of movie extras.

During warmer months, visitors arrive in a steady stream through-out the day, as families packed into cars, as groups filling tour buses, and as campers riding in motor homes. Some stay for just a short look, posing as ghosts emerging from the corn or standing beside the picket fence in front of the house they recall from the film. Others take a place in the outfield to shag balls for hours, losing track of time in a place where the ticking of a clock doesn't seem to matter. The spry bound across the infield dirt, crying with delight as they chase after baseballs. The pensive stroll along the edge of the cornfields vanishing into the rows and reappearing to a chorus of rustling leaves. The aged walk slowly around the bases, carefully rounding third and heading for home silently, buoyed by the constant chirping of birds and bugs. Some pose for silly pictures, re-creating a scene from the film or a baseball fantasy. Some sit quietly on the bleachers watching the proceedings. Some hug each other or hold hands. Some, experiencing more intense emotions, kneel and pray—or cry quietly.

In the guest book, emotions are capsulated in brief phrases scrawled in almost-reverent terms. A visitor from Sasayama City, Japan, wrote, "It took 12 years for my dream to come here. Today I did it." A Mid-westerner echoed, "It's the first time I've dreamed with my eyes open."

SHOELESS JOE COMES TO IOWA

Although *Shoeless Joe* is set in Iowa, many states and even Canadian provinces vied to attract the project. But after compiling photographs of a host of farms across the state throughout 1987, Iowa Film Office Manager Wendol Jarvis was able to offer what proved to be the ideal site. He brought the moviemakers to Iowa and set the stage for the Field of Dreams phenomenon. *Field of Dreams* director Robinson fell in love with the book *Shoeless Joe*, laboring for years to turn the fantas-tical story into a film, but it was a volunteer member of the Dubuque Film Board named Sue Reidel, serving as one of the bird dogs for film-makers, who discovered the Lansing farmhouse. (Reidel later worked selecting local actors for the film and arranging logistics for the film's baseball players, earning her a credit as "Iowa Casting Coordinator/ Bat Girl" for *Field of Dreams.*) Armed with a list of what Robinson was looking for, her own notes from reading W. P. Kinsella's description of the fictional Kinsella farm, and the picture from the cover of *Shoeless Joe*—which featured a view of a white farmhouse next to a red barn in a sea of corn much like the Lansing property or countless other Iowa farms—Reidel crisscrossed the Dubuque area logging many miles along back roads and snapping pictures.

The land around Dyersville had an ideal texture for the look Robinson was trying to achieve. The town has gentle hills to the east toward the Mississippi River, billiard-table flatness just a short drive to the west, and readily accessible picturesque small-town settings nearby. "A lot of it was the texture of the land and what felt right, also the look of some of the small towns," said Jarvis. "We felt that they could find more of the elements for the film here than anywhere else." The variety of topography and the proximity to towns that could double for Boston, Massachusetts, and Chisholm, Minnesota, made the Dyersville area an ideal setting for the film, but filmmakers still needed to find a farm that could be the focus for the plot line.

When she finally came upon the Lansing land and farmhouse, Reidel saw something she liked. "I thought it looked like the one on the book cover," she recalled. While she may have been sold, the people interested in bringing the film to Iowa still had to convince the filmmakers that they should come to make their picture in Dyersville. A site visit did the trick.

Robinson and other moviemakers set out to find the image that would be synonymous with "farm." On a cold day in February 1988, they found it just outside Dyersville. "I had certain criteria in mind." Robinson said. "I wanted something that was isolated from other farm houses so that you wouldn't have to answer the question, 'What do the neighbors right over there think of what's going on?' I didn't want something with a big silo that made it look like a wealthy megafarmer lived there. And it had to have a flat area right near the house that you could put a baseball field on, and yet we also wanted the house up on a little rise just because photographically it's more interesting."

Even though the Iowa countryside was flat and yellowed and missing its lush green corn when Wendol Jarvis brought Robinson and executive producer Brian Frankish to Dyersville, Robinson immediately took to the site. "Stop the car," he said as the vehicle drove down Lansing Road. "That's where I want to make my movie."

The location decision was made on site and quite eloquently. "I remember when we went to see it," Robinson said. "It was the first day of snow in Iowa. We stood there and it started to snow, and I remember saying to someone, 'On this ground, let us build a ballfield.'"

For Don Lansing, then a forklift operator at the John Deere factory in Dubuque who tended his farm after work, Hollywood's knock on the door was unexpected. A robust man with his parted dark hair often slightly tousled, Lansing is reserved, speaking slowly and deliberately. "It was the farthest thing away from my mind. It caught me totally off guard," Lansing recalled. "I said, 'What are you dreaming?' Usually the only person that knocked on my door was a salesman or a bill collector." After a bit of convincing and some negotiating, Lansing decided that his farm and farm house were ready for celluloid immortality.

When green in the summer, the location was already a postcard, with its little white house and faltering red barn standing out against a grove of evergreen trees in a sea of crops and fields under the expansive Iowa sky. The site turned out to be not only picturesque but very camera-friendly. The Lansing farm met the criteria for the film—a cozy, one-man farm with a two-story white farmhouse set off by a long driveway surrounded by cornfields and rolling hills. The small bridge over the creek that led from the road to the house would have to be reinforced to handle the traffic of moviemaking vehicles and equipment. A few other changes would have to be made. But the element that clinched the deal would definitely stay. The orientation of the Lansing farm meant that the baseball diamond in the cornfield would be perfectly situated between the farmhouse and the setting evening sun. That was what finally brought Hollywood to Dyersville. When told that the sun would set perfectly over the outfield corn with the diamond placed next to the Lansing farmhouse, Robinson knew he'd found his location.

The Lansing farm charmed Robinson and filled his needs, but by meeting one of the criteria to serve as the fictional Kinsella farm, the Lansing land almost missed its chance at stardom. The farm was definitely isolated. In fact, the farm was almost *too* isolated. The bird dog that first saw the land's star qualities could not find the farm on a return trip. Only after showing photographs to Dyersville residents was she able to find her way again to the future site of the Field of Dreams. Once she found the site, she also found out a little about Dyersville hospitality. Because he worked during the day, Lansing left his farmhouse door unlocked so that the location scouts could wander freely through his home.

Joseph and Catherine Lansing purchased the land on which the Field of Dreams sits in 1906. The farmhouse seen in the film was added in the following years. A Depression-era map of Dubuque County shows two hundred acres of Iowa farmland cut by a creek belonging to Jos. Lansing just outside the town of Dyersville. In 1939, son LaVerne and his wife Bernice purchased the farm. Don Lansing, grandson of Joseph and Catherine, was born in the picturesque white farmhouse in 1942 and purchased the farm from his parents in 1979. For eighty-two years, the Lansing farm was a quiet corner of the world where crops grew and livestock grazed.

In the summer of 1988, Universal Studios turned the Lansing home and farm into a back lot. Almost overnight, the Lansing property was transformed into the home, farm, and magical baseball diamond of fictional farmer Ray Kinsella. The farm's grain bin was removed and the driveway received a new layer of rock. The farmland was tiled—a subsurface drainage system was installed—so the land would dry quickly and so the film-related foot and vehicle traffic would not tear up the sod.

The house received a fresh coat of white paint, a white picket fence, and new bay windows. The front porch of the farmhouse was enlarged and a porch swing was added. A few interior walls were torn down and a few rooms were rearranged to allow the director to stage his scenes.

While the house was easily transformed, the lush acres of corn experienced a bit of stage fright. Filming was to begin in June, but an oppressive drought left the crop lagging. The film's producers resorted to insuring the cornfield to offset the disaster that would result if the corn failed to grow. Filmmakers even prepared to order fake corn. After all, as was the mantra, "No corn, no movie."

But, aided by the cooperation of the state of Iowa, the moviemakers dammed a nearby creek to create a reservoir—dubbed Frankish Lake after the film's executive producer—to provide the corn with enough water to coax it to its proper height. Perhaps the trick worked a bit too well. For one of the scenes when Kevin Costner as Ray Kinsella hears "the voice," he actually had to walk on a foot-high platform to avoid being dwarfed by the towering stalks.

To make a proper baseball field, the filmmakers had to extend their encroachment into the corn and onto the farm of Lansing's neighbors, Al and Rita Ameskamp. (The Ameskamps bought their land from Don Lansing's uncle in 1967.) This minor land grab was complicated by a fence that had to be removed and overhead power lines that had to be relocated during filming. The encroachment also meant that the corn crop could not be planted by each farmer on his respective property. The moviemakers hired a farm consultant, local farmer Eldon Trumm, to ensure that the corn was planted in uniform rows across the two properties. Trumm—a former mayor of the town of Worthington, just down the road from Dyersville, and a Hollywood veteran who helped teach Richard Gere to be a farmer for the 1988 film *Miles from Home*—can be seen in the film doubling for Kevin Costner in the wide shots of Ray Kinsella plowing under his corn to build the baseball diamond.

When the corn was finally the proper height, the time was right to build the movie set for the actual *Field of Dreams*. Four evergreen trees came down along with the acreage of corn. In came twenty-eight truckloads of dirt to help even out the undulating land for the ballfield. Over the four days of the Fourth of July weekend, the corn gave way to dirt, sod, and chalk as the construction team (aided by area high school baseball teams) created what would become a movie icon. It may have started out beautiful, but it took Hollywood magic to keep it that way. To make a pleasing color on the screen, the infield dirt was supplemented with crushed brick. Moviemakers confessed that they actually touched up the turf with some green vegetable dye and latex turf paint to keep the dying grass green as the filming schedule took its toll on the still-adjusting sod.

Filming continued for sixty-eight days through the long, hot summer into August 1988. The powerful klieg lights that illuminated the Lansing and Ameskamp farms during evening filming created a glow that was visible for miles across the flat Iowa countryside. While filming took place during the summer months, fake snow and blowers were needed to create Christmas in summer for one short scene involving Costner looking wistfully out the window at the not-yet-magical field in winter. Filmmakers actually used a matte painting to show the snowy baseball diamond itself. On another occasion, an obliging Iowa fog created the perfect setting for one eerie view of the field in the mist.

Some filming took place outside Dyersville. Dubuque doubled for Boston except for the scenes at Fenway Park, and Galena, Illinois, filled in for "Moonlight" Graham's Chisholm, Minnesota. But the Field of Dreams itself and the Lansing and Ameskamp farms had true star power.

Dyersville residents, including Don Lansing, his sister Betty Boecken-stedt, and Rita and Al Ameskamp, played roles as extras. Lansing and family members can be seen watching Kevin Costner build his ballpark and observing Amy Madigan as Ray Kinsella's wife, Annie, halting the spread of neofascism in America at the PTA meeting.

These roles had an unintended consequence as the Ameskamps, Lansings, and other local participants in the filming confessed that they cannot appreciate the film for its artistry or even concentrate on its plot while viewing. They find themselves distracted remembering watching the scenes as they were being filmed or remembering where they stood as the cameras rolled.

Hollywood's product may seem magical on screen, but it was long, hard work during filming. Watching the filming up close, Don Lansing said, "I found it interesting, but I thought it was dragging."

But Al Ameskamp enthusiastically said, "I had a ball. "Every spare moment I had, I was down here."

The Lansings, the Ameskamps, and most of their neighbors all participated in one of the film's most involved sequences. For the climactic scene, nearly all of Dyersville played a role. Responding to a newspaper advertisement, about 1,500 residents got in their cars and lined the road from the Field of Dreams out to the highway to portray the first visitors arriving at the field.

With the entire surrounding community darkened by a voluntary blackout that eliminated all outdoor lighting, and with each car tuned to a local radio frequency and taking directions relayed from a Universal Studios helicopter, the final scene came alive. As actors Kevin Costner and Dwier Brown engaged in the father–son catch that would soon reduce grown men to tears, the Dyersville extras drove in a procession to the field, turning their high beams off and on to create the twinkling lights that shimmer to the horizon as the film closes.

FANTASY BECOMES REALITY

When *Field of Dreams* stars Kevin Costner, Amy Madigan, James Earl Jones, and Ray Liotta left Dyersville, Lansing and the Ameskamps assumed life would return to normal—or maybe to normal with a few changes. Lansing's sister Betty wanted at least one change to stay after she saw the debut of *Field of Dreams*. "I just remember when we walked out of there, I told Don and Al, 'You cannot plow up that ballfield.'— not really even entering my mind that people would come," she said. "I just thought it was so beautiful. It was so pretty in the movie."

When the moviemakers removed the rented porch swing, Lansing bought another one to replace it, but he certainly did not expect the film to have much more of a lasting effect on his life. After deciding that he preferred the baseball diamond as it was to Hollywood's plans to restore his land to its prefilming site, Lansing resolved to maintain it as a baseball diamond for a time to enjoy a family ballgame or community function on the Field of Dreams. Betty remembered, "Don was going to have the neighborhood ballgame here and have family ballgames."

Field of Dreams executive producer Brian Frankish saw more for the former movie set than neighborhood ballgames. "I turned to Al Ameskamp and Don Lansing at the end of the picture, and I said, 'Hey, guys, I've got money here in this budget to restore your properties to the way that we found them, and I wouldn't be in too much of a hurry, guys, to do this. There's something very special about this picture, and this baseball field is going to have an opportunity to have a life here.'"

But Frankish returned from Iowa to Hollywood to finish work on the film, leaving Ameskamp, Lansing, and the field behind. As filmmakers readied a final product for the silver screen, only a handful of people even knew the soon-to-be-famous field existed. When summer turned to fall and then winter, there was very little reason to believe that the Ameskamp and Lansing land would become notable for anything except bushels of corn.

Dubuque hosted the world premier for *Field of Dreams* on April 20, 1989. Dyersville lost out on that privilege, but with its alluring ballfield, Dyersville has generated far more worldwide attention that its much-larger neighbor. The Field of Dreams soon ranked as one of Iowa's most notable attractions.

Just as the fictional Ray Kinsella unexpectedly found the fictionalized "Shoeless" Joe Jackson waiting in left field, on May 5, 1989—just weeks after the *Field of Dreams* world premier—Don Lansing noticed a man in a New York Giants hat standing along side the baseball field movie set. "I walked down to meet him," Lansing recalled, "and he stated he had just seen the movie and wanted to see the field before

I plowed it up." Others may have visited the field, unnoticed, but the man in the Giants hat was the first individual Lansing encountered on his land, moved by the film to come to Dyersville and the Field of Dreams. This first visitor, on his way from New York to California, left the black hat with the orange "NY" as a memento. The hat from a long-departed team that still tugs at fans' heartstrings was an apt metaphor for a former movie site that created a tug of its own.

When Lansing left for the John Deere factory each day, he placed a few leftover "I was in the 'last shot'" souvenir buttons near the field just in case more visitors stopped by. He also left a coffee can for donations. Day after day he would return to find a few buttons missing and the coffee can full of money.

Soon local and then national media reported on the pilgrimage, spreading the word of the field's growing fame and encouraging more visitors to set out for Dyersville. There were not yet signs on the road to direct visitors to the Lansing farm, and there were no pretty brochures for the site in the racks full of tourist information, but by the end of 1989, Lansing estimates that more than seven thousand visitors had made the trip up Lansing Road to the Field of Dreams.

Al Ameskamp was certainly not expecting that kind of reaction. As winter ended in 1989, he began plowing for the season's crop. After significant hesitation, he continued his plowing, returning the Field of Dreams' left and center fields to rows of corn. Built solidly, like an aging football coach who had thickened slightly around the middle, Ameskamp spoke with a touch of sentimentality as he recalled his decision. "I worked my way to the spot where the baseball field still lay sprawled out and open," Ameskamp said. "I just shut the tractor off and kicked my feet up on the dash and thought to myself a while. Should I or shouldn't I? In '88 the movie was shot, and in '89 it's time to go back to farming. So I dropped the plow down and took off right across my outfield portion of the ballfield."

Ameskamp did not have to wait to hear a reaction from fans of *Field of Dreams*. His wife gave him an early review. A former waitress with a bouffant hairdo and an infectious friendliness that would perk up even the most surly diner customer, Rita knew right away that reseeding the Field of Dreams was a mistake. "I said, 'Oh, m'gosh. People might like to see where the movie was made,'" she recalled, divining that her land would soon play host to visitors from afar. But even dismembered, with corn grown over much of the outfield, the site attracted visitors who left Al and Rita Ameskamp notes asking them to restore the field.

Lansing, too, had his doubts about keeping the field in the early days of the ongoing pilgrimage. Frustrated with the crush of attention focused on his formerly quiet corner of the world, he fretted about his visitors. "The way I'm beginning to look at it is, maybe keeping it was a mistake," he said in a 1989 *New York Times* article. "It is sort of getting out of hand."

Luckily for those who have been moved by their visit to the field, Lansing refused to let any momentary exasperation convince him that tending to the unique attraction was more trouble than it was worth. "I guess I'm keeping the dream alive," he concluded.

Brian Frankish—who more than a decade later could brag that he foresaw that the Field of Dreams would become an icon—noted with pride, "Everything that I thought about it, it has become." He recalled his final exchange with the man who plowed up part of the Field of Dreams: "Al Ameskamp, when I left, he says, 'Y'know Brian, I know what you're talking about not plowing up the field. Now, Brian, I'm a corn farmer. I grow corn. It's been great working with you folks, but I gotta go back to farming corn.' I said, 'Al, you gotta do what you gotta do, and if left field and center field gotta turn back into corn, that's your business.' So four months later I get this phone call, 'Hey, Brian, I'm getting a lot of pressure here from a lot of people.'"

Looking over his land a decade later, Ameskamp recalled, "I put a little box over there, and they put notes in it. I never received a snotty note." Instead, Ameskamp received pleas of "Please put the field back," "We love it," and "We wish it were there—all of it."

Ameskamp was moved by the pleas of visitors and touched by the stories of family reunions at the field, wedding parties seeking the field's blessings, and people who arrived to sprinkle the ashes of departed loved ones. Ameskamp restored the field to its pristine state for the 1990 baseball season. He even received some help from the Iowa Film Office to match the original crushed brick of the infield in the restored portions. "What changed my mind was when I started seeing so many people coming in to see the field and play on it just the way it was," Ameskamp said. The Field of Dreams was whole again and ready to receive its fans, sojourners, and pilgrims.

"I goofed it up one time," Ameskamp chuckled. "I made it right. Lord knows if I ever do it again, by God, I'd have to leave the country."

PEOPLE WILL COME

The former movie set was soon attracting visitors by the dozens each day—the casual visitor, the curious traveler, and even the occasional VIP. Baseball Hall of Famers George Brett and Reggie Jackson have visited the field to take part in special promotional games, as have actors Bruce Boxleitner and Jason Priestley. Baseball legends Lou Brock, Bob Feller, and Curt Flood have joined aging but enthusiastic ballplayers in a baseball fantasy camp conducted at the field.

In the Left and Center Field of Dreams gift shop, a map of the United States is decorated with colored pins placed by visitors. The Iowa–Illinois area is dense with pins, as are the major urban areas of America. Cards surrounding the map have been left by visitors from India, Italy, Spain, Venezuela, and the Czech Republic. This worldwide popularity is confirmed by the Field of Dreams Movie Site guestbook's entries from Belgium, Sweden, and Australia. The Field of Dreams even developed a special following in Japan, where baseball is popular and ancestors are revered. Buses filled with Japanese tourists make regular visits to Dyersville.

Field of Dreams played to enthusiastic crowds in Japan, and the movie site has been featured in Japanese publications and is paid tribute by numerous Japanese websites. Japanese home run king Sadahura Oh made a special trip to the Field of Dreams to film a commercial, changing from a business suit into a uniform in the Lansing house and watching much of *Field of Dreams* in the Lansing living room.

As word of visitors to the Field of Dreams spread, its notoriety was expanded by a flurry of global media attention. Touching stories of people seeking magic in the corn and fun anecdotes about festivals attended by former major leaguers were attractive material for journalists. American newspaper articles from coast to coast and mentions in the foreign press inspired many to make the trip to Dyersville. Features on television news programs brought the field alive in countless living rooms, and a film about the field and its visitors premiered on the cable sports network ESPN and was screened in the Baseball Hall of Fame theater. The Field of Dreams was soon mentioned prominently in travel books, pamphlets, and guides. It was even declared one of the "Top 10 Lawns in the Country" by lawnmower maker Briggs and Stratton.

The number of visitors to the Field of Dreams roughly doubled each year from seven thousand to fourteen thousand to nearly thirty thousand. Even though hard numbers are elusive since the field has no fees and issues no tickets, it is estimated that each year the field now draws between fifty thousand and seventy thousand visitors.

In a May 1992 account of the economics of the Field of Dreams, *Chicago Tribune* reporter David Young noted that while attendance is not recorded at the field, the National Farm Toy Museum saw an increase in annual attendance from about eighteen thousand in 1989 to fifty thousand in 1991. Based on the assumption that approximately half of the visitors to the Field of Dreams visit the Toy Museum, Young concluded that the former movie set drew approximately sixty-five thousand visitors just three years after the debut of *Field of Dreams*.

Phil Robinson, who has not returned to Dyersville since the completion of filming, first heard media reports about the life-imitates-art phenomenon of the field's tourists, then received a call from the

Ameskamps with the interesting news. When told of the continuing throngs that make the trip more than a decade after the debut of *Field of Dreams*, he uttered a wistful "unbelievable," amazed at the large numbers of people who continue to be affected by his work and its physical remains.

The parade of outsiders—initiated by the film and encouraged by the media accounts of those who traveled to the field—has been an economic boom for Dyersville. According to the Iowa Film Office, Hollywood spent more than $3 million in Iowa while filming *Field of Dreams*. The Dyersville Area Chamber of Commerce further estimates that the average visiting family of three staying overnight spends $158 per day in the small town. But serving as stewards and tending to the visitors responsible for this impact creates a significant burden.

Brian Frankish had advised the farmers to leave the field intact, suggesting it could become an attraction like the ranch that served as Southfork on the television show *Dallas*. But while the *Dallas* site attracted the curious, the Field of Dreams attracts people not only looking for a curiosity but searching for a form of peace. As an attraction, therefore, the Field of Dreams could not become a circus. Iowa Film Office manager Jarvis simply suggested that the farmers "do the best" and not cut corners and make sure that the field continues to appear how a fan of the film would want to see it.

Lansing and the Ameskamps did not set out to become Walt Disney. They were content to be farmers. But as more and more visitors turned up their drives, they had to make decisions: Would they tolerate signs directing visitors to the field, would they charge an admittance fee for visitors, would they allow groups to host games on the field, would they allow advertising signs, and would they sell souvenirs?

Looking back after a decade of trial and error as hosts to a million visitors, the Iowa farmers simply marveled at how far they have come. Questions about liability insurance and product licensing were just issues to work out along with decisions on when to cut the grass and when to plant the next season's corn. Al Ameskamp summed up his experience evolving from farmer to tourism professional: "You just go ahead and work things out." Had they paused each time to ask all the questions lawyers would ask—should people sign waivers to walk on the field, should the farmers work out a common maintenance schedule for the turf, and should the Field of Dreams have a mascot—Lansing and the Ameskamps may have never undertaken their unique responsibilities. But finding their own way, the neighbors have avoided destructive issues and have allowed the field to speak for itself and find its own audience.

The Field of Dreams experience soon included promotional brochures, souvenir stands, and, to accommodate demand, step-on guides for the many tour buses that visit the site. Betty Boeckenstedt took to managing the Field of Dreams Movie Site gift shop and its small staff. In Left and Center Field of Dreams, groups can arrange a special appearance by Ghost Players who will walk out of the corn to complete the *Field of Dreams* movie fantasy. But even with the embellishment and the addition of some commercialism, the field's allure has endured.

The field's tenders realized that the people who walked around their land were more than just curious tourists. They came for more than a photo opportunity and left with more than souvenirs. People in wheelchairs were pushed around the base paths, individuals walked the bases with the help of crutches, and elderly visitors, supported by loved ones, slowly paced the diamond. The field has hosted the first meeting of long-separated fathers and sons as well as countless family reunions. It has seen proposals and marriages—some visitors return annually to renew their vows—and has reportedly been sprinkled with the ashes of a former Major League Baseball player spread lovingly by his son around home plate.

Al Ameskamp recalled watching people so lost in their own thoughts that he could walk right past them while they stared into the corn and they wouldn't even notice anyone had passed. Don Lansing remembered watching the chance meeting of two estranged brothers who found each other by total coincidence on the former movie set. One visitor has returned again and again with a special mitt inscribed with the date of each trip on the glove's soft leather.

For actor Timothy Busfield—who in *Field of Dreams* portrayed Ray Kinsella's disbelieving brother-in-law Mark, who could not see the magic of the Field of Dreams and who threatened to foreclose on the mortgage for the Kinsella farm—the transformation of the field is clear. "What the field is to the audience and what the field was to us are two completely different things," Busfield said. "For us, it was a workplace; for the people it's a shrine."

James Earl Jones, who played reclusive writer Terence Mann, sees the field as something special for its visitors. "It's a place where people come to reconcile," he said. "It's a little sanctuary in a way."

Author W. P. Kinsella, who was bored by the filming process and left Dyersville after a brief stint as a reluctant extra, was captivated by interacting with the field as an attraction. Of his postfilming visits to Dyersville, Kinsella said, "I'm always thrilled to go there because I meet such interesting people who have come thousands of miles, sometimes all the way from Japan, to walk on the field, to play catch, to hit the ball, to just sit on the little bleachers and absorb the atmosphere."

Field tenders Lansing and Ameskamp have been astonished and tickled by their enthusiastic visitors—Lansing has even found a bride in a woman drawn to the ballfield she saw in her dreams. For those who traveled thousands of miles to walk on the field and search for redemption amid the rows of corn, for those who reconnected with family and found acceptance and escape on the exceptional bit of dirt and grass, and for the countless tourists who have been charmed by the simple pleasures of a day of leisure playing ball under the azure Iowa sky, the fertile patch of earth continues to have a powerful effect on visitors. These kinds of reactions are not typically associated with the average tourist attraction, but it is possible to venture some reasons for the field's unique attractiveness.

In *Cooperstown to Dyersville: A Geography of Baseball Nostalgia*, anthropologist Charles Fruehling Springwood examines how a point on a map can be transformed into a culturally significant destination. Springwood writes, "At the Field of Dreams, the site has been variously interpreted as a baseball narrative, a journey into the past, a celebration of boyhood, and a site of personal redemption."

More than just a tourist stop, this once-artificial place has grown to represent something very real to the people who have journeyed to frolic in the shadow of the Iowa corn. People visit destinations of cultural significance for many different reasons, but, as Springwood notes, "people's involvement with these sites is exceedingly meaningful, often ineffable, and nearly always *emotional.*" Visitors cannot always explain why they are moved to travel to the Field of Dreams, and while actual reactions depend on an individual's personal history and subjective interpretation of the site, the Field of Dreams has elicited responses from pleasant smiles to uncontrollable tears.

The voice told Ray Kinsella, "If you build it, he will come." Hollywood came to Dyersville to build a baseball field that would realize the vision created by the book *Shoeless Joe* for *Field of Dreams.* When Hollywood left Dyersville, that vision was more than an image on celluloid. The vision was real. As life has imitated art, a movie set has become a place where dreams and hopes can come true.

2

Life Imitates Art

"People will come, Ray. They'll come to Iowa for reasons they can't even fathom."

—*Terence Mann*

Becky DuBuisson's husband died in 1991. He was a baseball fan, a long-suffering Red Sox fan, and had viewed *Field of Dreams* together with Becky many times. After his death, Becky grieved. But when more than three years had passed, the sun began to shine again for her and she was able to begin to move forward with her life. Then Becky had the dream.

From Colorado, Becky dreamt of the Field of Dreams. Then the image of the field began to enter her waking thoughts, coalescing into an idea. The idea compelled her to be at the Field of Dreams at midnight on New Year's Eve eating a hot dog and drinking a root beer.

More than a century before Becky had her vision, music teacher William Pitts stopped in a small town about seventy-five miles northwest of Dyersville. While waiting for his stagecoach horses to be changed, Pitts wandered the streets. He stopped in a particularly scenic area and imagined that a church would look just perfect in the picturesque setting. Inspired by the scene, he wrote a poem about his imagined church that he set to music. The song spoke of his "little brown church in the vale." Upon returning to the spot years later, Pitts was stunned to discover that a small church was actually being constructed on the site he

envisioned years before. It was even painted brown. Pitts found a copy
of his song and performed it at the church's dedication.

The new church was serenaded with praise: "There's a church in
the valley by the wildwood,/No lovelier spot in the dale." More than a
century later, Pitts's "little brown church in the vale" attracts visitors
who come to enjoy the charming scene of the tiny church among the
pine trees. Brides and grooms come to receive the church's blessings
and ring the church bell for luck. For Becky DuBuisson, the Field of
Dreams became her little brown church in the vale, and she hoped that,
just as Pitts's vision had been realized, the subconscious vision that
invaded her own dreams could become something tangible that could
help her continue her healing process.

In 1994, on a trip across the country with her aunt, Sheila Henning,
Becky had the chance to make her dream come true. She traveled to
Iowa where she visited the church in the vale and read the plaque dedicated to the church's builders to find the name of her late husband's
grandfather. She then came to Dyersville at the end of December to
find frigid temperatures and snow-covered fields, but she still wanted
to fulfill her mission. Once in town, she contacted Don Lansing,
who—after considerable prodding—gave permission for the later-
than-usual visit to his property. With the field covered in a few inches
of snow and freezing temperatures gripping the region, Becky enjoyed
her root beer and hot dog (because it had been purchased much earlier in the evening at the local Dairy Queen, it was by then a very cold
dog) and circled the bases of the snow-covered diamond to celebrate
New Year's Eve.

The next day, Becky and her aunt returned to thank Lansing for
his hospitality. Lansing, curious about his visitors, played at clearing
snow from his walk to size up the women who walked up the path to
his house.

"I want to thank you," Becky said.

"I've been waiting for you," Lansing responded, knowing his midnight visitors would come back.

Lansing invited his guests in for coffee, and the group spent hours talking. Days later, Becky returned to continue the conversation. She left a snow angel as a farewell note. Becky and Don developed a friendship. The forty-one-year-old widow and the fifty-two-year-old lifelong bachelor remained in contact.

Becky, an intense and wary woman with an infectious smile and an ability to open up to others almost unconditionally when she feels a level of trust and acceptance, returned to Dyersville for weekend visits, and the relationship turned from friendship to romance. Becky had clearly been affected by Lansing and, just as clearly, had also made a strong impression on Don.

In July 1995, Becky and Don walked around the field talking about the future. Lansing stopped at first base and proposed. They performed an instant replay at home plate to be sure they got it right. Becky DuBuisson and Don Lansing were married at the Basilica of St. Francis Xavier on February 10, 1996.

FICTITIOUS PLACES, GENUINE RESPONSES

In January 2001, a letter to the editor of *Sports Collectors Digest* responded to the question "Of all the game-used memorabilia . . . which ones do you prefer?" by declaring, "If I were to purchase one sports memorabilia item for my collection, it would be the ball used in the scene in the movie, '*Field of Dreams*,' where Kevin Costner was playing catch with his father. It is one of the best baseball movies of all-time and there is only one of those balls out there."

Many visitors to the Field of Dreams leave notes in the guest books declaring "great movie" or "loved the movie," affirming the notion that the desire to connect with the film provides much of the motivation for visitors who come to Dyersville. Some leave simple notes consisting of lines from the film talking about "going the distance" or asking, "Is this heaven?"

Once at the site, many people act out scenes from the film, disappearing into the corn and yelling, "I'm melting," or doing "the wave" on the bleachers. Others play out the fantasy as if they arrived on the morning after the end of the film as part of the line of cars shown in the final scene. They pose for pictures in front of the house and stare contemplatively at the players on the field.

Perhaps it should be no surprise that a movie locale can attract a crowd just like an art museum or historical site. Entire books and tour packages are devoted to the unique landmarks and attractions that dot the American landscape. People crisscross the country and the world not only to visit sites of historical or cultural significance but to commune with what has become familiar through popular entertainment. Millions visit the Smithsonian Institution's many museums for the collections of artifacts significant to the national consciousness. But in the Smithsonian's National Museum of American History, one of the most popular exhibitions displays memorabilia from film and television including the Fonz's *Happy Days* leather jacket and Dorothy's ruby-red slippers from *The Wizard of Oz*. The connection to the popular, established by its omnipresence and willingly accepted in broadcasts into everyone's living rooms, is able to outshine the connection of the notable and the distinguished.

The popularity of a nursery rhyme drove developer Robert McCullough to buy London Bridge and relocate it to Lake Havasu City, Arizona. Although McCullough apparently thought he was buying the more picturesque Tower Bridge, the rebuilt London Bridge not only is not falling down but is one of the state's top tourist draws and has inspired British-themed development in the surrounding area. A few hundred miles south, the notoriety of the gunfight at the O.K. Corral—enhanced by numerous reenactments on film—has brought travelers to Tombstone, Arizona, where sightseers not only can see the restored O.K. Corral but also can read the grave markers of the victims of the famous shootout in Boothill Cemetery.

Some wayfarers look to go riding five hundred miles on the *City of New Orleans*, while others look to get their kicks on Route 66. In Paris, fans flock to the grave of former Doors lead singer Jim Morrison. In

New York City, visitors climb like King Kong to the top of the Empire State building. In Philadelphia, people run up the Art Museum steps like Rocky Balboa. In Boston, tourists pose for pictures in front of the bar that served as the model for the television tavern *Cheers*. In Memphis, the faithful go to Graceland.

For many, these sites connect them with lost youth, remind them of memories of days gone by, or resonate as an absence where once there was such a powerful presence. Pop culture's ability to connect people from different backgrounds is more than a wistful verse; it is a verity.

The expanding reach of mass media culture is astounding. Brought into people's lives via radio, television, film, periodical, and Internet connection, these common experiences help individuals and society at large. In 1938, approximately six million American listeners tuned in to Orson Welles's radio broadcast of H. G. Wells' *War of the Worlds*. One Princeton University study estimated that 1.7 million of those listeners believed that Martians had truly landed in New Jersey. A staggering six hundred million viewers—about one fifth of the world's population at the time—watched astronaut Neil Armstrong take his first steps on the moon in 1969. More than 106 million viewers (60 percent of the American television-viewing audience) watched the final episode of the television show *M*A*S*H* in 1983. According to one survey, in 1998, 12 percent of all American adults or more than twenty million people used the Internet to access the Starr Report's tawdry tale of President Bill Clinton's dalliance with a White House intern. The entertainment and infotainment of the popular culture generate a tremendous attraction across gender, ethnic, and socioeconomic groups. Both accessible and compelling on such a large scale, pop culture extends its grasp in a way that can bring together kindred spirits separated by distances—and generations.

The concept of pop culture can be traced to the notion of *vox populi*—"popular opinion" or "the voice of the people." This idea has been transformed into "popular culture," used to describe the democratic culture of the masses as opposed to the culture of elite society. In the

1960s, this notion was further changed into "pop culture" to refer most specifically to the entertainment culture that is now omnipresent in everyday life. Unless one is living as a hermit, pop culture overlaps with every facet of modern life, providing the images and soundtracks that lurk in the backgrounds of everyone's existence and help shape American society's consolidated identity.

People like to be a part of a group, to belong. Futurist marketing consultant Faith Popcorn observed a modern variation of this theme and named the trend "clanning." By clanning, people seek the reinforcement of those who share their interests, values, and beliefs. By visiting sites of common interest, members of these loosely affiliated clans perform something of a ritual dance. Perfect strangers at the Field of Dreams quote lines from the film, spontaneously agree to rent a VCR and view the video, and cavort on the former movie set to reexperience the film and the emotions it generated. In this way, people both participate in a fantasy within a group and act on emotions as an individual.

As social animals, human beings just do not like to be alone. Religion is one connector that brings people together and creates a reassuring grasp on reality when the turbulence of life threatens to upset their psychological stability. Heritage is another connector that allows people the comfort of knowing that they are part of a group, linked to the past with a grasp on the present. But connections are not just forged through theology and genealogy or through high culture. People search for common denominators every day and are happy to be individuals as long as they know that there are others just like them to reinforce their sense of individuality. While it is in constant flux and therefore not as stable as established institutions like religion or ethnic heritage, pop culture can provide that connector. From fan clubs that bond enthusiasts, to chat groups that use modern telecommunications technology to link kindred spirits across the globe, to *Simpsons* key chains that proclaim an affinity for four-fingered, yellow animated characters, individuals express devotion to a collective life. As one indicator of the scope of this desire to bond with the familiar, consider that the *Licensing Industry Survey 2000* estimated that, for that single year, licensing revenues of entertainment and character properties equaled more than $2.5 billion—that is more than the annual budget of all but the largest American cities.

Ray B. Browne, the former director of Bowling Green State University's Center for the Study of Popular Culture, refers to pop culture as a "kind of secular religion." Especially in a culture that prizes the democratic ideal that all are created equal, the popular can cut across boundaries of class, ethnicity, and education. The rich and the not-so-rich can share a passion for professional sports. Individuals of different hues can find common interest in popular music. High school drop outs and Ph.D.s can share a water cooler discussion about a television situation comedy.

Fans seek to extend their connection with the object of their affection, whether it be a sports team, a film, or a cartoon. Some purchase merchandise; others join clubs or create tribute home pages on the Internet. By reading books about sports stars, fans are able to extend their connection to a favorite team. By visiting movie locales, fans are able to enhance their bond to a favorite film.

KINSELLA'S STORY

Field of Dreams gained its inspiration from W. P. Kinsella's *Shoeless Joe.* "I had read the book by W. P. Kinsella in 1981 or '82 and just immediately fell in love with it," said *Field of Dreams* director Phil Alden Robinson. "I thought it was the most original and wonderful and visual story I had read in a long time."

But Robinson's affection for the book made him want to maintain the story in its entirety. "I love the book *Shoeless Joe* passionately," he said, "and really set about with great trepidation adapting it to a movie because I knew that you had to make some changes." He wanted to be sure that his changes met with the approval of the book's author.

Robinson wrote to Kinsella, saying, "I want you to like what I am doing because I am so in love with this book." But according to the director, Kinsella was unfazed. "He sent me back a postcard which just said, 'Dear Phil, do whatever you have to do to make it a movie. Love Bill.'"

With the author's approval, a now-confident Robinson produced his screenplay and set about translating Kinsella's vision onto celluloid. Kinsella's early reviews were very positive. Recalling his reaction, Kinsella said, "When I read the screenplay, I had tears in my eyes and I thought, 'My gosh, this is my own work that's doing this to me. If they can translate this screenplay onto film it can't help but be wonderful.'"

When he finally saw his vision on the silver screen, Kinsella was delighted. "I'm thrilled with the movie," he said. "I thought they did a wonderful job of it. I don't see how they could have done a much better job."

That didn't mean that the director was satisfied. Robinson fretted during the entire filming process over whether he was capturing the spirit of the book he was so passionate about. "All the time we were making it, I wasn't enamored of it, and when we cut it together, I thought, 'Hmmm, I don't know if it works,'" he said. "It wasn't until we started showing it to people and they were responding to it the way I responded to the book did I feel that we'd gotten it."

In the end, the artist was able to finally step back from the canvas with a smile on his face. Looking back, Robinson said, "It delivered what I hoped it would deliver, which is what the book did for me."

Even though the filmmaker followed the book's basic formula, the film could not retain all of the book's complexities. Kinsella's original narrative is a rich tale of the near-religious aspects of baseball and a compelling story of one man's attempt to use the national pastime to connect with his deceased father.

Kinsella is a member of the Society of Baseball Research, whose disciples are known for their exhaustive study of baseball data that sometimes reduces the fun of "take me out to the ballgame" to the chore of solving a quadratic equation. Reading his almost-reverent description of the national pastime, one might believe Kinsella to be a fanatical aficionado bent on self-immolation in the baseball commissioner's office to protest the scourge of the designated hitter, or a zealous fan holding season tickets behind home plate, screaming about a player's inability to lay down a sacrifice bunt in a crucial situation. Kinsella is neither. Of baseball, he says, "I'm not a fanatic. My feeling for baseball is a little like Cordelia's statement to King Lear [in Shakespeare's play]. She said she loved him as a daughter loves a father. No more and no less."

In fact, Kinsella confessed that he never really played baseball as a kid. Kinsella's father played minor league ball, and the author was weaned on baseball stories, but he did not see his first baseball game until he was eleven and did not attend his first major league game until age thirty. Growing up in Alberta, Canada, Kinsella was far removed from the constant exposure to baseball most American kids receive. But Kinsella's father would read him accounts of baseball games, and the two would share in the experience of a live big-league game by listening to the All-Star Game or the World Series broadcast on Canadian radio. When asked how he was first inspired by baseball, Kinsella answered, "My dad talked a good game."

The bespectacled author with flowing, straw-colored hair, thick mustache, and occasional full beard looks more like an aging Buffalo Bill Cody than a baseball old-timer. Seeing photographs of the wiry Kinsella at the plate on the Field of Dreams, black socks in sandals planted in an unsteady stance, back shoulder dropping as he readies to take a swing, it is not difficult to believe his confession "I don't play the game; in fact, I throw like a girl." Maybe a below-average ballplayer but a superior writer, he describes the secret of writing fiction as the ability "to make the dull interesting by imagination and embellishment, and to tone down the bizarre until it is believable."

As the epigram for *Shoeless Joe*, Kinsella chose a quotation from Bobby Kennedy: "Some men see things as they are and say why; I dream of things that never were and say why not." Kinsella certainly enjoys dreaming of things that never were and making his fantastical visions believable. But he demurs when describing his ability to make the unbelievable come alive. Instead, the author cites a groundedness as the secret to his success. "I think in order to write of the fantastical you have to have an extraordinary grip on reality."

While Kinsella denies that his stories are autobiographical, he does tuck a piece of himself in his works. Many of his baseball tales are set in his beloved home away from home, Iowa; refer to the Pioneer Rookie League that plays through Montana and into Alberta, Canada; and slyly include a tidbit that recalls another Kinsella work—an inside joke to true fans, encouraging them to mine for other Kinsella nuggets.

Kinsella spins enchanting yarns with engaging concepts like long-dead Chicago Cubs fans pleading with God to allow their team to win the last pennant before Armageddon; Roberto Clemente washing ashore—unchanged—after twenty years ready to resume his baseball career; a tied baseball game that runs on into thousands of extra innings and stretches the boundaries of time; a baseball league established for talented players who play petrified of choking in a pressure situation; and, of course, "Shoeless" Joe Jackson emerging from the Iowa corn. "Being accepted as a baseball novelist is like striking a vein of gold," Kinsella stated. "When one strikes a vein of gold, one does not abandon it until every last nugget is mined."

The book on which *Field of Dreams* is based won much praise from the literary world and became a staple on the library shelves of serious and casual baseball fans alike. Sports participant–author George Plimpton called *Shoeless Joe* "a strong candidate for any literary Hall of Fame."

Considering how his baseball literature would eventually be regarded, it is intriguing that Kinsella's *Shoeless Joe* was actually born of somewhat humble origins and was not clearly destined for publishing's major leagues. The book was originally a short story titled "Shoeless Joe Jackson Comes to Iowa." Of the story's genesis, the author stated, "I was living in Iowa City, Iowa, and I got to thinking of some stories my dad had told me about the Black Sox scandal. And my dad was a bit of a storyteller, so they were good stories but they weren't necessarily true stories, and I just thought, 'What would happen if "Shoeless" Joe

Jackson came back to life in this time and this place which was Iowa City, Iowa, in 1978?' And that was the beginning of the novel."

The fantastical story of the baseball outcast being summoned from the Iowa corn caught the eye of an editor at Houghton Mifflin, who contacted Kinsella and asked him to expand the idea into a full novel. At first, unsure that he would be able to take on such an ambitious project—the short story was the longest work Kinsella had ever attempted—the author incorporated other notions into his tale, and it blossomed into the book that inspired the film and the foundation for the resulting pilgrimage to Dyersville.

Kinsella's *Shoeless Joe* hit the shelves with the promise that "the power of dreams can make you come alive." Into his novel, Kinsella incorporated the story of Archibald "Moonlight" Graham, whose real-life appearance in a single major league game Kinsella always found intriguing. He also added a story about a man who claimed to be the oldest living Chicago Cub based on Kinsella's real-life encounter with a man who made the same representation. He included the exploration of the life of writer J. D. Salinger, whose self-imposed literary exile Kinsella found fascinating for the fact that Salinger made himself conspicuous by hiding. The original short story (retained as a first chapter) and the other narratives intertwined to create the story that became the basis for *Field of Dreams*.

In the book, W. P. Kinsella's Ray Kinsella character has a twin brother Richard (a yin to Ray's yang) who left home after having a falling out with their father. As copied for the film, the Iowa farmer hears the voice—the voice of a baseball announcer, not an ethereal whisper—and builds the magical baseball field that calls forth the ghosts of Joe Jackson and the 1919 White Sox. Ray Kinsella follows the voice's guidance on a cross-country journey and returns to the field with true-life reclusive *Catcher in the Rye* author J. D. Salinger, incarnated as a fictional character for the book; the young version of Archibald "Moonlight" Graham, the one-inning major-league-veteran-turned-doctor; and Eddie Scissons, the man who claims to be the oldest living Cub.

As in the film, the farm faces foreclosure, Karin nearly chokes, and the cars signify the beginning of the progression to the field. In Wizard of Oz–like fashion, Salinger finds his rapture as he follows the ghosts into the corn; Archie Graham realizes his dream to get a major league at-bat; Eddie Scissons sees a young version of himself make true his false claim of Chicago Cubs lineage; and Ray Kinsella, joined by long-lost twin Richard, reconnects with his father. The compelling story weaves a tale of baseball and fantasy and suggests that people can make their dreams come true, have second chances, and use the universality of baseball to form bonds they don't have the words to produce.

For *Field of Dreams*, director Robinson combined the twin Kinsella brothers into a single character who agonizes over growing old and turning into his father, while harboring a regret that his father passed away before their father–son conflict was resolved. This neatly wraps the twins' character into a single figure and sets the stage for the drama of the final scene with a climax that is lacking in the book. Readers are introduced to Kinsella's father before the end of the novel, and the father–son reconciliation is foreshadowed. The ending is a surprise for film viewers in a way that effectively achieves its emotional response.

In the final version of *Field of Dreams*, the story of the oldest living Cub ends up on the cutting-room floor, as does a subplot involving a semievil plan to eliminate the independent farmer through the creation of computer controlled megafarms. Kinsella's wife Annie becomes a more fleshed-out character who is affected by the magic of the voice in her own dream and a more pronounced participant in her husband's activities. The PTA meeting scene where Annie passionately argues against book burning while defending the Constitution and the Bill of Rights is added as a way to develop her character while introducing viewers to the fictional Terence Mann. The Mann role, written specifically with James Earl Jones in mind, evolved as a conscious effort to avoid any legal action by J. D. Salinger's lawyers. The tall, white, and good-humored fictional Salinger from *Shoeless Joe* would not be confused with the large, black, and surly Terence Mann.

The film also alters the timing of the story, setting the tale at the end of the eighties. This change makes farmer Ray Kinsella a child of the Woodstock era (the book's Ray Kinsella may have been a little too old to get the full Woodstock experience). The resulting generation gap between the farmer and his father resonated with the legion of baby boomers who lived through that turbulent time and finally gained an understanding of some of their parents' burdens when they raised their own families.

MIXED REVIEWS

In "Reel Sports," a 2001 *Sports Illustrated* article about sports films, Jack McCallum writes, "Every time a ballplayer materializes out of the damn corn in *Field of Dreams*, I get a migraine (one Hollywood writer calls the movie *Field of Corn*), yet Oliver Stone, no sentimentalist he, says he loves the film and 'the way it evokes *The Wizard of Oz.*'" Similarly, when *Field of Dreams* debuted, it was not at all apparent that the film would be successful, let alone inspire any global pilgrimages.

Field of Dreams opened to mixed reviews. *New York Times* reviewer Caryn James concluded that the film "leaves little room for ambivalence. Audiences will probably believe in Mr. Costner's illusion or not, love or hate this film."

In *The New Yorker*, Pauline Kael's review opened with a broadside on the film, the presidency, and an entire generation: "*Field of Dreams* is a crock—a kinder, gentler crock. If the Reagan era was Eisenhower II, this picture could be construed as the opening salute of the Bush era: Eisenhower III. (Baby boomers talk counterculture and vote conservative.)" Instead of the power of dreams, Kael takes from the film the message that challenging your parents' values will make you sorry. After questioning the director's intentions, the use of the stars, and an authenticity-straining combination of elements, the review declares, "This whimsical fantasy isn't just removed from all reality, it's removed from its own subject matter. . . . The kick of the game is missing."

Roger Angell similarly did not care for the film, writing, "It was a Sara Lee chocolate layer cake, with icing so thick that I could feel it dripping onto my shoes." Angell even went through the effort of listing famous baseball players who never played catch with their fathers and never missed it—including Ty Cobb, Ted Williams, and Lou Gehrig—to debunk the notion that playing catch with Dad is a right endowed by the Creator like life, liberty, and the pursuit of happiness.

In *Time, Field of Dreams* was derided as "the male weepie at its wussiest." *People Weekly* questioned the film's believability: "The more you think about it, the more deceived you'll feel." *The New Republic* was a bit more caustic, noting, "There's never any question of believing the story; for a while there's a chance of accepting it as a means to sentiment, but it all collapses quite early." *The Nation* declared, "It gives wish fulfillment a bad name." One writer in *Film Comment* chastised the film for heavy-handed religious proselytizing, charging that director Robinson has made Joe Jackson a Christ figure whose second coming will enable believers to be saved.

A scan of the popular print media outlet reviews runs the gamut from pans to praise. Boos cascaded in from *Rolling Stone, Film Comment,* and *New York.* But publications like *Variety, Newsweek, Los Angeles Magazine, National Catholic Reporter,* and *Philadelphia Magazine* provided more favorable treatment.

Playboy suggested, "*Dreams* is a disarming fantasy if you go with it, though literal-minded moviegoers may feel someone has thrown them a wicked curve." The Canadian *Maclean's*—perhaps pleased with the success of the Canadian-born author of *Shoeless Joe*—lauded, "They have captured the mercurial spirit of Kinsella's novel and added an emotional grandeur worthy of both Hollywood and baseball." *Cosmopolitan* suggested, "Director Robinson and superstar Costner have managed to shape this farfetched scenario into a fantastically warm, wacky, and wonderful event."

In *Commonweal,* reviewer Tom O'Brien remarked, "It's the kind of film that either nauseates or works on its own terms." He criticized the

"embarrassing ode about the all-American goodness of baseball," noting the film missed the opportunity to have the black Terence Mann
take Major League Baseball to task for not integrating until 1947. He
similarly wondered whether the lack of Negro League veterans walking
out of the corn—could it be that baseball heaven had yet to break the
color barrier? (Looking back, the film's director agreed and confessed,
"I didn't give enough thought to it. It was a mistake on my part. I
should have. I kick myself for that. I should have done it.") Finally,
O'Brien wondered whether the Joe Jackson character could have been
more honest about the errors in judgment he displayed in his role in
the Black Sox scandal. While O'Brien confesses to having rolled his
eyes a few times, in the end he was thrilled.

Venerable baseball writer Steve Wulf was a fan, claiming, "*Field of
Dreams* combines illogical elements to produce a gem of a baseball
movie." Even though he, too, found fault with what he dubbed the
"sentimental rhapsody to baseball," Wulf forgave the lapse and decided
that the film transcended the baseball movie genre. He concluded,
"*Field of Dreams* is not for everyone," but advised anyone who enjoyed
It's a Wonderful Life or *The Pride of the Yankees* to run to see the film.

In the Canadian magazine *Cineplus*, W. P. Kinsella added his own
praise. While reviewing the film based on his own book may have been
an odd glance in a fun-house mirror, Kinsella took gingerly to the role
of film critic. "As I watched the movie *Field of Dreams* for the first time,
it was an eerie feeling to see the characters from my novel, *Shoeless Joe*,
come to life on the screen."

Kinsella praised, "Like the novel, the movie is not about baseball but
is a gentle love story with baseball unobtrusively in the background. The
film captures the dreamy quality of the novel, the lush Iowa cornfields,
the steamy warmth of Iowa summer nights." In the end, after subtract-
ing points because he felt that Timothy Busfield's performance as Ray
Kinsella's disbelieving brother-in-law Mark was not villainous enough
for his taste, and that Ray and Annie's daughter did not look enough like
Kevin Costner and Amy Madigan to appear as a convincing daughter,

Kinsella gave *Field of Dreams* four stars out of five and warned that the film came with a four-handkerchief ending.

The author's approval aside, some baseball purists were dismayed to see Ray Liotta's right-handed plate appearances as the lefty Jackson. Jackson actually batted left and threw right while Liotta threw left and batted right. Few complained that Liotta as "Shoeless" Joe Jackson wore shoes—Jackson earned the nickname when, as a young ballplayer, he took off ill-fitting new spikes to play in stockinged feet—but some questioned why Jackson's uniform looked so pristine. The 1919 Chicago White Sox were not called "Black Sox" because of the scandal but because they refused to pay White Sox owner Charles Comiskey twenty-five cents to clean their uniforms and elected instead to play in dirty uniforms. Nitpickers wondered how, as a true baseball fan, Ray Kinsella's character could walk out on the game between the Red Sox and Athletics in the fourth inning. People who put way too much thought into the matter wonder whether a reincarnated Joe Jackson, who proclaimed his innocence in the Black Sox scandal, would really take to the field again with the ringleaders of the conspiracy to throw the 1919 World Series.

Director Robinson actually was quite conscious of the fact that some would be thrown because actor Ray Liotta played the part of Joe Jackson from the wrong side of the plate. He reasoned that because the vast majority of those who would see the film never actually saw Joe Jackson play, they would not have an image in their mind of what Joe Jackson looked like as a player and therefore would not necessarily be as jarred by Liotta's portrayal as they would if they saw an actor playing Ted Williams as a righty. "We were being inaccurate," he confessed. "But we were not running up against a strongly held image that would have really been a bump for a lot of people."

As far as those who press the issue, Robinson noted the irony of critics who accept the premise of the film—that a long-dead baseball player can be reincarnated in an Iowa cornfield—yet complain about the fact that the film's Joe Jackson is a righty at the plate. The director chided simply, "He was an illiterate from the south; we've got him reciting poetry with a Jersey accent. It's fiction."

Field of Dreams struck a chord with men who long for improved relations with their fathers or sons and moviegoers who happily suspended their disbelief hoping that dreams can come true. The film has had an enduring fame. From April through October 1989, *Field of Dreams* grossed more than $62 million domestically. Internationally, *Field of Dreams* grossed an additional $16 million. Domestically and internationally, *Field of Dreams* videocassette rentals generated an additional $32 million and $8 million, respectively. The film was a commercial hit and has been described as a classic of modern American cinema.

Of course, as the artist who brought the story to life on film, Robinson continues to angst over the final product years after *Field of Dreams* debuted. "I'd reshoot it all tomorrow if I could," he confessed. "There isn't a scene in the movie where I think that I got it."

If the director still harbors doubts about his work, his executive producer foresaw the film's powerful potential from his first read of the script. Brian Frankish recalled looking over the tearjerker ending and knowing that the film would create a powerful response. "When I first read the screenplay," he said, "we used to say that the last ten pages of the script were printed on onion paper. It was the finest screenplay I had read in my career up to that time and may still be."

Tim Busfield is a passionate baseball fan who still plays competitively for a semipro team. But it was the magic of the script, not the film's ties to baseball, that attracted him to the project. "I read the script, and the second I opened the first page it was almost like fairy dust came kicking off the title page," Busfield said. "It was just a magical script."

Busfield's role in the film is complex because, although he plays a character that does not believe in the magic of Ray Kinsella's field, his is a character that viewers can use to relate to the plot. "I'm kind of the audience's route into this movie," he said. "I let them into the movie a little bit because I'm on the disbelieving side—for them to believe they have to kind of go past me."

But while his character may deny the magic, Busfield is certain that such enchantment must be possible. According to the actor, "A child has to work out his relationship with his parents, inevitably, and there's just no way around it. If you've got a fractured relationship, or if it's altered or cut short for any reason, I think the powers that be will make it happen for you whether in this lifetime or the next. I buy the whole thing. Sure, I buy the whole thing."

Once he was finished with *Field of Dreams*, Busfield moved on to other projects but was conscious of the news that his former movie set became an unlikely tourist destination. "My first reaction was, 'How weird, really weird, that anybody would do that'—and sort of, 'How sad,' because to us it was a movie location," he said.

But he had an opportunity to return to the Field of Dreams to record the phenomenon surrounding the pilgrimage for a CBS World Series broadcast. Upon his return, witnessing firsthand the emotional bond between the field and its visitors, Busfield's view was transformed. "There were kids crying who had come back because their dad had died and it was his favorite place and he was a baseball fan," he recounted incredulously. "People had gleaned some magical, mystical experience from the field, which was not at all what I experienced—it may have been what other people in the movie experienced—but not what I experienced while we were filming it. Nor did I experience it when I went back there. To me, it was just a movie set. It would be like having a mystical experience going on the Warner Brothers lot. It just wasn't going to happen. But I was shocked, and by the end of the day I couldn't believe what people were experiencing. It was mind-boggling, and it still is mind-boggling."

As for why the film resonated so well—especially for men— Busfield has a theory involving the film's score. According to Busfield, "There's a note that James Horner hits in his music about the time when Kevin's character says to his dad, 'You wanna have a catch?' There's a note that he hits that's like the dog whistle for men's emotions. It sets off something that men, the emotional side of men, just lets go."

For actor James Earl Jones, concentrating on his craft kept him from making any predictions about the film's success. "You're doing a story, and you're doing it the best you can," he said. "You are doing it to please yourself. You're doing it to fulfill the concepts you might have about excellence or about accuracy or about fulfilling the imagination. That's all you can do; you can't have a sense of how it's going to work out."

But Kevin Costner had an idea that he was making something special while filming *Field of Dreams*. "I think the movie stands a chance to not only become a classic but represent to this generation—my generation—those things that *It's a Wonderful Life* did to previous generations," Costner said in an interview conducted near the end of filming.

"It's a movie that dared us to take risks with it," Costner said. "It could have boiled over and been schmaltzy and been dismissed. Or it could walk that fine line and be really cool, and take hardened people like us and make us buy into the movie, so that suddenly *we* want somebody to be out on that baseball field as badly as Ray does."

While making *Field of Dreams*, Robinson understood that the conventional wisdom in Hollywood was that a film could not succeed by pushing baseball or farming. But with then-emerging star Kevin Costner lending credibility as the film's protagonist and a message that spoke to aging baby boomers, it clicked.

Nominated for three Academy Awards, including best picture, best screenplay based on material from another medium, and best original score, *Field of Dreams* missed out on Oscar glory (*Driving Miss Daisy* won best picture and best screenplay adaptation; *The Little Mermaid* took home best original score), but the millions of people who enjoyed the film did not seem to mind the slight. The film earned Robinson significant professional acclaim, including the distinction of "Screenwriter of the Year" from the National Association of Theatre Owners.

With the perspective of the passage of time and a view of the film's significant following, *Field of Dreams* has overcome some of its less-than-enthusiastic reviews to achieve a lasting legacy. After bestowing four stars on *Field of Dreams*, film critic Roger Ebert concluded:

> The director, Phil Alden Robinson, and the writer, W. P. Kinsella, are dealing with stuff that's close to the heart (it can't be a coincidence that the author and the hero have the same last name). They love baseball, and they think it stands for an earlier, simpler time when professional sports were still games and not industries. There is a speech in this movie about baseball that is so simple and true that it is heartbreaking. And the whole attitude toward the players reflects that attitude. Why do they come back from the great beyond and play in this cornfield? Not to make any kind of vast, earthshattering statement, but simply to hit a few and field a few, and remind us of a good and innocent time.

LIFE IMITATES

Near the end of the film, as the Kinsella farm faces foreclosure and the Field of Dreams faces destruction, Ray Kinsella is told that the farm's salvation will be visitors who will gladly pay to visit his baseball field. It is Kinsella's young daughter Karin who first declares, "People will come." She goes on to articulate a vision that visitors will find their way to the Kinsella farm and pay for the privilege of watching the enchanted game on the magical field.

The older, wiser Terence Mann expands the vision as the film's drama comes to its climax:

> People will come, Ray. They'll come to Iowa for reasons they can't even fathom. They'll turn up your driveway, not knowing for sure why they're doing it. They'll arrive at your door, as innocent as children, longing for the past. "Of course, we won't mind if you look around," you'll say. "It's only twenty dollars per person." And they'll pass over the money without even thinking about it, for it is money they have and peace they lack.

And they'll walk out to the bleachers and sit in shirtsleeves on a perfect afternoon. They'll find they have reserved seats somewhere along one of the baselines, where they sat when they were children and cheered their heroes. And they'll watch the game. And it will be as if they dipped themselves in magic waters. The memories will be so thick, they'll have to brush them away from their faces.

"It's a lovely speech," said Robinson, "and he reads it so beautifully, and you say, 'That's a beautiful image.' But there's a part of you that doesn't really believe it's going to happen. Which is why that ending is still such a surprise. I get goosebumps when I see it, when those cars start showing up."

How to actually deliver the speech was a question that had to be resolved during filming. It had to be believable and convincing, but not evangelical or overblown. Jones confessed he did not try to oversell the message but rather wanted the words to speak for themselves. "I didn't get into character. I just said to Phil, 'I can proclaim this like an orator or a poet, or I can just simply say it,' and he said, 'Let's just say it.'" The reading obviously had a powerful effect and resonated quite clearly in those for whom baseball is a powerful connector.

"He made a choice," said Robinson. "He said, 'I don't want to preach in this scene; I don't want to be too big.' He said, 'I just want to play it simple and conversational.'"

The fictional speech from the film, which echoes a similar recital from the book, has proven eerily accurate even if it is, on its face, somewhat unbelievable. Robinson confessed that, as a reader of *Shoeless Joe*, he thought the idea of people driving up to the Kinsella farm ready to pay for the privilege of looking at the magic ballfield was hard to accept, but he offered, "That's what made it such a wonderful surprise at the end when they did come."

It is fun for the reader and viewer that they did come in the book and the film. It is even more intriguing that they did come in reality. But to talk simply of a life-imitates-art response to the speech from the film is to severely narrow the discussion. Life and art seem to entangle in all facets of this charmed project.

The "people will come" speech was a story unto itself. In fact, the speech was the reason James Earl Jones signed on to the project. It was actually Jones's wife who was first attracted to *Field of Dreams* and the role of Terence Mann. "My wife read the script before I got home, and she handed it to me and said, 'Jimmy, you've got to do this movie,'" Jones recalled. "She said, 'Of course the long speech about baseball—they'll cut and it'll end up on the cutting room floor, but you still have to do this movie.'" That prophesy turned out to be incorrect, and the speech that launched the entire life-imitates-art phenomenon remained in the final version of the film.

But before filmmakers decided to visit Dyersville, some of this magic was already milling in the Iowa corn. In August 1987, a year before Don Lansing would even learn about the *Field of Dreams* film project, his uncle Herbie paused, considering the land surrounding the Lansing farmhouse. He said, "Donny, this would be a nice place to have a ballfield." At the time, the land was just a hay field, but Herbie could see it as a place for family gatherings and ball games. Thanks to one director's vision, Uncle Herbie got his wish.

Robinson wrote his screenplay in 1983, but he truly had to go the distance to see his adaptation make it to the silver screen. Twentieth Century Fox was originally going to make the film but dropped the project after four years of work, fearing it would not be a commercial success. Prior to *Field of Dreams*, Robinson's only major directorial effort was the box-office disappointment *In the Mood* (he would go on to direct *Sneakers* in 1992 and the television movie *Freedom Song* in 2000). When he finally received the go-ahead to make *Field of Dreams*, Robinson had his work cut out for him. "This movie had a profound impact on me," Robinson said. "I never cared so deeply about anything. I had a comfortable budget, a great schedule, not to mention some of the biggest actors around. The producers told me, 'OK, you've been wanting to do this thing for seven years, so go do it.' Now that's pressure." With

Universal Studios behind the project, *Shoeless Joe*—as the film was originally titled—was finally ready for lights, cameras, and action.

The name *Field of Dreams* itself has an enchanted origin. After much
discussion, Universal Studios officials decided to change the name of
the film from *Shoeless Joe* to *Field of Dreams* as a way to entice moviegoers beyond baseball aficionados who would know of the banished
outfielder. As a fan of the book, Robinson had been set to maintain
author Kinsella's original title. At first, Robinson was disheartened.
Looking back, he thought *Field of Dreams* sounded like the name of a
room deodorizer.

But when Robinson called to inform Kinsella of the news of the
name change, the author was unconcerned. Robinson recalled, "He
said, 'Oh, I don't care about that. That was never my idea for the title
of the book anyway; the publisher came up with that.' I said, 'Really,
what did you want to call it?' He said, 'I wanted to call it *Dream Field*,'
and I hadn't said '*Field of Dreams*' to him yet at that point, and when
he said that, I thought, 'Don't argue any more; this is a *Field of Dreams*
moment. The universe has opened itself up and showed itself to you
for a few seconds just like Ray Kinsella saw it, so just keep your mouth
shut. Accept it. That's the new title.'"

Just as the enchantment of Ray Kinsella's magic field neatly tied the
loose ends for the fictional characters, the decision to rename the film
neatly realized the author's original vision. The film and the movie site
that would become the pop culture mecca had their common name.
Chicago's Wrigley Field might be referred to as the "friendly confines,"
but only "Field of Dreams" advertises its attraction with its title.

The life–art Ping-Pong match continued throughout filming (which
began on Robinson's father's birthday) and into the movie site's afterlife. In character, Kevin Costner took advantage of a break while bored
between takes to carve "Ray Loves Annie" in a heart on the bleachers.
Visitors can still find the tribute to a fictional love on the top row of
the small stands just off the first base line. In Galena, Illinois, where the
Field of Dreams crew filmed the scenes set in Chisholm, Minnesota, a

Civil War monument dedicated "to the soldiers of Jo Daviess County who served in the War of the Rebellion 1861–1865" stands in Grant Park, named for former general, president, and Galena resident Ulysses S. Grant. Among the names of the men Jo Daviess County sacrificed for the good of the Union is a young man named John Kinsella, the same name as fictional farmer Ray Kinsella's father.

Details seen in the film tangle life and art as well. The actors and actresses of *Field of Dreams* may look to be perfectly cast, but they weren't necessarily the only choices for the roles. Kevin Costner, still an emerging star when *Field of Dreams* was cast, had to compete with established stars like Jeff Bridges, Robin Williams, and Jack Nicholson for Universal Studios' attention. In the end, what director Robinson termed a "Gary Cooper–like" quality earned him the chance to bring the role to life. Jimmy Stewart had been Robinson's first choice as "Moonlight" Graham, but Stewart passed on the opportunity, and Burt Lancaster was cast. Early in *Field of Dreams*, Ray Kinsella orders Karin to turn the television off, perhaps irritated that it is showing a film about a man many considered to be insane. Karin is watching *Harvey*, which stars Jimmy Stewart as a man who talked to a six-foot tall invisible rabbit. The scene is included in *Field of Dreams* in tribute to the great actor.

Of course, it was after the film reached its audience that the fictional idea of people traveling to Iowa to visit a baseball diamond in a cornfield became real. In the book, the first visitors to arrive at the Kinsella farm come in a "black Chrysler with the scorched-gold license plate of New York State." The first Field of Dreams visitor Don Lansing encountered on his farm was a New Yorker wearing a New York Giants hat. (Incidentally, Lansing drove the first car to the field in the last scene of the film.) Life and art continued to trade volleys from there.

Television producer Tim Crescenti created a documentary about the phenomenal afterlife of the *Field of Dreams* movie site. The video *Dreamfield* debuted on ESPN in 1994 and "picks up where Hollywood left off." On-screen anecdotes of people sharing sentimental reunions in the corn are just a hint of the behind-the-scenes story of the making of the video itself.

Crescenti, who at age thirty-one was a former coordinating producer for the television show *Love Connection*, had tired of the drudgery of setting strangers up on dates to create television magic. As he was looking for direction in his professional and personal life in 1993, he came across an article in the *Los Angeles Times* about the continuing charm of the Field of Dreams.

"I was just expecting to lay out in the cornfields and look to the heavens and get some sign from God on what I was supposed to do for the rest of my life," he said, describing his vision for his journey to Dyersville. But once there, he met other visitors and was inspired by their various motivations to seek something at the former movie site.

"Universal Studios came and constructed a baseball field and has had this powerful effect on people from all over the world," he remembered and wondered, "How can this field have this effect on people?" He had found an inspiration and some direction in his life and career. Inspired by his visit to the field, Crescenti was moved to capture the shrinelike appeal of the former movie set.

The idea incubated for a time while Crescenti worked on another project, but then, without any real studio or financial backing, he decided to move forward. He began setting up interviews and throughout the summer of 1994 brought together people with interesting stories at the Field of Dreams so he could film a series of interviews.

The project was not without its own challenges. Before his deal with ESPN was complete, Crescenti and his wife had been financing the project by running up debt on their personal credit cards. Like Ray Kinsella, Crescenti's pursuit of his dream threatened him with financial ruin.

Another challenge was convincing a much-in-demand James Earl Jones to narrate the story. Like the fictional Iowa farmer who convinced the reclusive writer to participate in his fantastic voyage, Crescenti pitched and pleaded, finally convincing the actor to tell the story.

But after Jones had signed onto the project, a hectic filming schedule threatened to derail his involvement. Crescenti had to travel across the globe to South Africa where Jones was on location for the 1995 film *Cry, the Beloved Country* to tape narrative footage.

As Terence Mann, Jones declared that people would come to the field. As narrator of *Dreamfield*, Jones told the story of how life imitated art. But instead of simply documenting how truth can be stranger than fiction, the *Dreamfield* project recalled Ray Kinsella's fanatical pursuit of an unbelievable dream. Jones described Crescenti as a "real-life Ray Kinsella," which could make the *Dreamfield* video life imitating art to create art to illustrate life imitating art. To add a final twist, portions of *Dreamfield* even appear on the collector's edition of the *Field of Dreams* DVD. In the end, the film about the phenomenon is art after all.

The art of *Field of Dreams* has even helped extend and expand real lives. In *Field of Dreams*, Archibald "Moonlight" Graham lives out his dream to step up to the plate as a major leaguer through the magic of Kinsella's enchanted field. Those fans who rushed to *The Baseball Encyclopedia* can attest to the fact that "Moonlight" Graham—Archibald Wright Graham—did indeed play in one major league game for the 1905 New York Giants. Fictionalized by W. P. Kinsella for *Shoeless Joe* and then brought to life by Burt Lancaster in *Field of Dreams*, the true-life Graham was much like his literary and film equivalents.

W. P. Kinsella actually traveled to Chisholm, Minnesota, to perform research for his book and found "Doc" Graham to be a pillar of the community. While the 1905 New York Giants went on to win the World Series, Graham became a doctor after seeing a single half inning of major league action. He settled in Chisholm, where he spent the next forty-four years as physician for the Chisholm schools and gained recognition for a landmark study of children's blood pressure. Graham died in 1965, leaving behind his wife Alecia and the legacy of a generous and community-minded figure. Author Kinsella returned home from Chisholm with a poignant story of a man who could have been expected to be bitter or regretful but instead moved on to live a rich and full life. Delighted by his experiences in Chisholm, Kinsella inserted Veda Ponikvar, founder of the *Chisholm Free Press* and real-life author of Graham's obituary, as a character—herself—in *Shoeless Joe*. In her tribute entitled "His Was a Life of Greatness," Ponikvar wrote of Graham, "For the old and the young of this little mining town who knew Doctor Graham . . . his era was an historic, unique sort of legend. There will never be another quite like it."

"Moonlight" Graham's transformation from the most minor of footnotes in baseball's record books to fictionalized notoriety created a cult following for the half-inning hero. While few may remember Lee Graham or Peaches Graham—the two players who bookend "Moonlight" Graham in *The Baseball Encyclopedia*—millions know the man who left the baseball field to become a small-town doctor. It is Graham, the character who could have spent a lifetime brooding over what could have been, who expresses the notion that there is a time to embrace the future and leave the past behind.

In the film, Burt Lancaster as "Moonlight" Graham suggests, "We just don't recognize the most significant moments of our lives while they're happening."

"In some ways," said Robinson. "I thought that was the most important line in the film." It underscores the importance of enjoying a lifetime while it is being lived, not regretting chances of a lifetime once they are passed—a central message of Kinsella's book and Robinson's film.

That message has resonated with many *Field of Dreams* fans and has compounded life's imitation of art in Graham's adopted home. The town of Chisholm took stock of what was important to its citizenry and its collective civic conscious. Like the rest of the world, Chisholm rediscovered its suddenly-famous resident and decided to commemorate his life by changing the name of a local park from "Paradise City" to "Paradise City—A Field of Dreams" in honor of the major-leaguer-turned-doctor. Town residents went further and created a Doc

Graham Memorial Scholarship, awarded to two deserving Chisholm High School graduates who demonstrate a commitment to community service. That scholarship is now partly funded through the sale of newly minted "Moonlight" Graham baseball cards.

There is even a notion—popularized by one of the Graham Scholarship Fund baseball cards—that "Shoeless" Joe Jackson may have actually met "Moonlight" Graham in real life.

According to the former president of the old Mesabi Baseball League and the uncle of the cocreator of the Doc Graham Memorial Scholarship Fund, "Shoeless" Joe played in the Mesabi League under an assumed name after he had been banned from baseball in 1920. The league, named for a Minnesota mountain range, played through Chisholm, where a young-at-heart but aging Graham played baseball in another league. Maybe it is just wishful thinking of imaginative fans, but perhaps the meeting between the man shunned by baseball and the man who dreamed of batting in the big leagues actually took place, not in film or fiction but in a long-gone Chisholm ballpark.

Helping complete the life–art–life circle, Dyersville's Ghost Players have journeyed from the Field of Dreams to Chisholm, where they posed for pictures on the steps of Graham's former home. The Ghost Players donated the use of their image to raise money for the Scholarship Fund, and the scholarship cards are sold at the Field of Dreams souvenir stands. According to Mike Kalibabky, cofounder of the Doc Graham Memorial Scholarship Fund, each television airing of *Field of Dreams* creates a spike in card sales—aided by an accessible Internet site promoting the cards—as the interest in Graham's real-life career peaks.

If interest in the book *Shoeless Joe* and the film *Field of Dreams* resurrected the long-forgotten fame of "Moonlight" Graham, it has fortified the resolve of "Shoeless" Joe Jackson fans who believe that the legendary outfielder belongs in the Baseball Hall of Fame. Of course, Jackson's career statistics—a .356 lifetime batting average, the third best in baseball history, and twelve seasons hitting above .300, including a .408 average in 1911—would place him among baseball's elite.

However, having been banned from baseball by Commissioner Judge Kenesaw Mountain Landis for his participation in the conspiracy to throw the 1919 World Series, Jackson waits in baseball purgatory for his chance to join the game's immortals.

Even though the real Joe Jackson could not read or write while in the major leagues, the fictionalized Joe Jackson of *Shoeless Joe* and *Field of Dreams* is an eloquent speaker who talked passionately about his love of baseball. In *Shoeless Joe*, the fictional Jackson declared, "I loved the game. I'd have played for food money. I'd have played free and worked for food."

In the film, Ray Liotta as Joe Jackson describes his longing for baseball: "Getting thrown out of baseball was like having part of me amputated. I've heard that old men wake up and scratch itchy legs that have been dust for over fifty years. That was me. I'd wake up at night with the smell of the ballpark in my nose, the cool of the grass on my feet—the thrill of the grass." The fictionalized character's eloquence, profound affection for the game, and sense of personal loss have energized Joe Jackson fans and inspired a new generation of supporters to take up the disgraced outfielder's cause.

A number of nonfiction books about "Shoeless" Joe Jackson have been published since the debut of *Field of Dreams*. A "Shoeless Joe Committee" and a "Shoeless Joe Jackson Society" have pursued the goal of having Jackson inducted into the Baseball Hall of Fame. Even baseball immortals such as Ted Williams and Bob Feller have lent their names to these efforts.

The residents of Greenville County, South Carolina, followed the example of Chisholm residents by renaming a playground and dedicating Jackson's boyhood field as Shoeless Joe Jackson Memorial Park to recognize their favorite son. A South Carolina highway is now named the "Shoeless" Joe Jackson Memorial Parkway to memorialize the former baseball star.

Intriguingly, during the same baseball season that *Field of Dreams* debuted in 1989, Pete Rose was banned from baseball for allegedly betting on major league games. Dubiously linked together by their banishment, Jackson, Rose, and their respective fans look toward the possibility of a second chance to earn redemption for posterity. Even though Jackson received his fictionalized amends in literature and film, both he and Rose await the ultimate reparation—induction into the Baseball Hall of Fame in Cooperstown, New York.

Neither *Shoeless Joe* nor *Field of Dreams* foretell enshrinement in the Hall of Fame for Joe Jackson (or Pete Rose), but fans must wish they had, since both book and film have proved to be eerily prophetic. From predicting the real-life pilgrimage to Dyersville to divining the state from which the first visitor would travel, art associated with the *Field of Dreams* has had an excellent record of anticipating life.

PLAYING HOST

In *Shoeless Joe*, before he experiences the magic of the Field, the J. D. Salinger character challenges Ray Kinsella, "If you've got what you say you have out there in Iowa, then it shouldn't be hidden. You're making thousands of people unhappy. It's like hoarding the secret of eternal life." The Salinger character then semiseriously imagines visits to the field being conducted in clandestine fashion for a chosen, privileged few: "At dawn every day there would be private planes leaving New York, Washington, D.C., Los Angeles, and Miami. Cedar Rapids Airport would have to build new runways to handle the traffic. Of course it would all be very secretive, the pilots wearing dark glasses, fake mustaches, military uniforms."

Sensing he has struck a nerve, Salinger presses Kinsella about the possibility that the magic field could become overly commercialized. He challenges, "In the winter, you'll sell hot apple juice and cinnamon, and postcards, and little plaster statues of Shoeless Joe Jackson with a halo over his head. You wouldn't mind all that, would you?" Kinsella protests that he would never allow his special field to become something crass.

The Field of Dreams' tenders have faced similar challenges. The fence that had divided the Ameskamp and Lansing lands may have been torn down to create the Field of Dreams, but the issue of how to best present the field created a less visible, but often perceptible, neighborly divide.

A destination that attracts visitors creates demand. Visitors need shelter and sustenance—and souvenirs. For Dyersville, a town that suffered recent losses in the manufacturing industry, hospitality-related jobs help provide employment for the local workforce. Bowing to demand (visitors had been appropriating ears of corn and handfuls of grass from the property) and seeking to help subsidize the operation and maintenance of the field, Lansing first, and then the Ameskamps, opened small souvenir stands on each of their properties. Keith Rahe founded the Ghost Players in 1990 to bring to life the fantasy of old-time ballplayers emerging from the corn and interacting with visitors. The neighbors collaborated for years on a Field of Dreams festival that attracted former major leaguers and overflow crowds to Dyersville. But as the pilgrimage continued, the pressure to expand the Field of Dreams experience and capitalize on the influx of tourists created a rift right along the Lansing–Ameskamp property line.

The farmers who own the land on which the field sits had never been tourism professionals and never aspired to be much more than welcoming while trying to retain their respective sanity as the seemingly endless flow turns up their driveways. The Lansings and Ameskamps sometimes struggled to deal with this pilgrimage.

If tens of thousands of people each year showed up on the average American family's lawn, taking pictures through living room windows and tromping through the flower beds, that family would be hard-pressed to figure out an appropriate response. The tenders of the Field of Dreams struggle with an appropriate way to acknowledge the pilgrimage, provide hospitality to the visitors, and maintain their privacy—and sanity. They have to make decisions about the types of uses they would allow for the field and the kinds of souvenirs they would sell, and they had to answer a variety of questions about their unique attraction. As the years went by some issues were resolved and new ones presented.

In 1996, after deciding that the demands of visitors exceeded the ca-
pabilities of their "mom-and-pop" operation, Al and Rita Ameskamp
moved from their farm to a nearby town. They leased left and center
fields to a limited liability corporation that contracted with the Ghost
Players' Keith Rahe to manage the Ameskamps' portion of the field.
Under Rahe's stewardship, Left and Center Field of Dreams has welcomed guests with batting cages (since closed) and a corn maze to provide a bit of fun to go along with the magic of the corn. Still under the
care of Don and Becky Lansing, the house and farm, infield, and right
field have more or less been allowed to speak for themselves.

Differences are manifested in subtle ways. Visitors are asked to leave
the Field of Dreams Movie Site (the Lansing side) after 6:00 in the
evening. Visitors to Left and Center Field of Dreams (the Ameskamp
side) are permitted to remain until dusk. The Ameskamps have encouraged the Ghost Players to put on their "Greatest Show on Dirt" on
the last Sunday of each month. "People come here to fantasize," said
Ameskamp.

The Lansings question whether the role play prevents some visitors
from enjoying their own private Field of Dreams experiences and have
relegated the Ghost Players to the Ameskamp land in left and center
fields. "This field isn't about ghosts," said Lansing. "It's about everybody having some little dream, what they want to get out of the field.
. . . When the ghosts are performing, people can't even walk around."

While in past years the field has been used for corporate outings, political appearances, and product commercials, such activities are now
rare. In recent years, the stewards of Left and Center Field of Dreams
have been more open to outside uses and other activities, allowing the
experience to expand beyond a simple preservation of a movie set; the
Lansings have generally sought to preserve the field as is so individual
visitors can interpret it in their own way.

W. P. Kinsella has been saddened to hear of the friction between the
field's owners. "It's too bad that they can't get along because I think
they both sort of want the same thing," he said. Offering his own take

on how he would proceed if the unique attraction were located on his own land, Kinsella commented, "I would go by the book, by my book. If I owned the property, I'd be charging $20. After all, this is America."

So tourists may not understand why two separate driveways and two separate signs invite them to the field; late-arriving visitors may not understand why they can only frolic on part of the field; visitors who borrow equipment from the Left and Center Field of Dreams souvenir stand are encouraged to restrict the use of the bats and gloves to the outfield; souvenir seekers must choose whether to make their purchases from the red-painted, barnlike stand on the Lansing property or the vinyl-sided cabin on the Ameskamp property. (The new cabin replaced a quaint red hut resembling a railroad caboose that formerly held the Ameskamp's souvenir stand.)

But these issues go unnoticed by the vast majority of visitors. They see the Field of Dreams as one entity and happily cross the Lansing–Ameskamp property line as they chase balls or flirt with the edge of the corn. The invisible property line creates no more of a distraction to the average visitor than the shadow of the power lines (restored along the property line since the completion of filming).

In the end, the Field of Dreams has not declined into a playground for a chosen few. It has not become about well-heeled visitors enjoying a private spectacle or rich fans enjoying a tour of a private game reserve or baseball safari. It is an open and unpretentious pickup game that goes from dawn to dusk, involving the athletic and the awkward, the young and the young at heart, and the mainstream and the marginalized.

Many visitors have come for the irresistible pictures and pose walking in and out of the corn or having a catch like in the film. But as life has imitated art, the site has become a destination, but not only for tourists who are visiting large balls of twine and other eccentricities or for curious fans who want to see tangible evidence of a favorite star or film. The former movie site has become a draw for people looking for something simple in a hectic world, for individuals who seek the sacred in the secular world, for many hurting souls who hope that the field can be a catalyst that can help them achieve their own personal redemption, and for a population of baseball fans looking to use the national pastime to help mend personal bonds or remind them of a time when they believed it was just a game.

3

Where Time Can Stand Still

"This field, this game . . . it's a part of our past, Ray. It reminds us of all that once was good and it could be again."

—*Terence Mann*

"What we seek to do now is an act of faith," began the local magistrate to commence the marriage ceremony. In an act of faith, however, Jerry Ryan and Lynn Burke chose not a church or a courtroom but a former movie set.

Jerry and Lynn married at the Field of Dreams on a perfect summer's evening on September 1, 1989. The pair had been dating for two years, both refugees from unhappy first marriages. On a date earlier that year, they saw *Field of Dreams*. As a baseball fan, Jerry was amazed by the film. Lynn was not as passionate but grew to suspend her disbelief and find enthusiasm for the fantastical story. On a camping trip months after seeing the film, Jerry saw an article in a newspaper about Dyersville's Field of Dreams and the thousands of people who visited it. "He said, 'If I were to marry again, it would be at that field,'" recalled Lynn of the unlikely pseudoproposal. "I looked at him and thought he was completely crazy. I said, 'A ballfield in Iowa?' I said 'You are crazy.'"

While Lynn wasn't completely sure whether the offer was serious or even sane, Jerry saw a quality that he wanted for himself. "When I saw the movie, the place struck me as a perfect place," he said. "If I was going to get married again, I wanted to get married in the most beautiful place I could."

The pair set off on the lengthy road trip from Rochester, New York, to Dyersville, Iowa, not exactly knowing what would occur. Jerry suggested that if they could travel well together, it would be a sign that they could get along well enough to make a life together work. However, fourteen hours into the trip, that life together changed dramatically. As Lynn drove on a highway near the town of Lagrange in northeastern Indiana, a truck hit their van.

The truck seemed to come into the vehicle through Lynn's window, and the van careened down the highway, spinning wildly. When they finally came to a stop, Jerry and Lynn were not sure they were still alive. In the aftermath of the crash, the van was crumpled, littered with broken glass, and stained with blood.

Miraculously, Jerry and Lynn walked away from the harrowing accident with only minor cuts on their elbows, but the van was totaled. Cool under pressure despite frayed nerves, Lynn took charge of the postaccident logistics, dealing with the insurance company, police, and tow truck operator. Jerry was so impressed with her demeanor under such trying circumstances that he formally proposed right there in the junkyard near the wrecked van.

The couple arrived at the Field of Dreams shaken by their traumatic experiences but excited about their intent. Under a shining sun, they saw people playing on the Field and met Don Lansing. Happy to be alive after the accident and thrilled to be at the Field of Dreams, Jerry introduced himself to Lansing with a straightforward greeting. Jerry said, "My name is Jerry Ryan. I've driven here from New York. We just survived a very bad accident, and I just have one question for you: 'Is this heaven, or is this Iowa?'—and I was serious."

Jerry recalled that Lansing gave the enigmatic answer, "It's whatever you want it to be."

For Jerry and Lynn, the Field of Dreams was about to become the site of their wedding. If Lynn was befuddled by the notion, her first view of the diamond changed her mind.

"We pulled up at the Field of Dreams about three o'clock in the afternoon," she said. "It was a very mystical feeling. It was as if we were walking into heaven itself." The well-tended field on a pleasant day, filled with children and adults playing catch and running the bases, suddenly seemed like an ideal wedding location.

At first, Lynn had been a little tickled and excited with the idea of seeing the former movie set and experiencing, in person, what she had seen on screen. Once there, she saw her destination for more than its association with the film. "I felt very relaxed at the field, and I knew I was a part of a very friendly human experience," Lynn said, feeling like a part of the Field of Dreams clan. "Everyone had a story to tell and had traveled many miles.

"It's just humanity and love and communication; you were absorbed by it. My best word for that, when I'm at that field, [is] I feel magic and I feel humanity. I was absorbed by that feeling."

They approached Don Lansing and told him of their interest in using his baseball cathedral as a wedding chapel, content to marry in their traveling clothes. Dyersville hospitality, however, would not hear of it.

Between Friday night and Saturday evening, the people of Dyersville helped arrange a wedding gown—complete with all the necessary alterations—as well as a cake and the last tuxedo in town. Of course, the last tuxedo in Dyersville was a perfect fit. That's just the way things seem to go at the Field of Dreams.

Jerry dressed in the Lansing farmhouse, and like the fictional Ray Kinsella, he looked out over the ballfield in the corn wondering whether the field had magic in store for him. The Lansing farmhouse also served as Lynn's bridal chamber and so she strode, flowers in hand, past the porch swing and onto the field.

From out of the corn, the burly, bearded groom emerged in full, traditional black tie to meet the perky, fresh-faced bride in her newly tailored gown. Jerry and Lynn met at the pitcher's mound and walked together to home plate where a magistrate from Dubuque waited with Don Lansing, who served as best man. In the glow of the Iowa twilight, on the land where Kevin Costner and Ray Liotta brought W. P. Kinsella's novel to life, Jerry and Lynn became husband and wife.

Dozens of townspeople attended the ceremony, brought gifts and champagne, and joined in the celebration. The happy couple cut their wedding cake and celebrated with new friends beneath a poster of Kevin Costner from the film. The magical night ended with a somewhat less-than-magical honeymoon as Jerry and Lynn slept in their rental car in an airport parking lot waiting to catch their 7:00 A.M. flight back to Rochester.

Much as the unconventional honeymoon suite helped bring the Ryans back to Earth after their enchanted nuptials, the bliss and excitement of the wedding at the Field of Dreams faded into everyday married life. The couple was blessed with a daughter, Mary, when the 1991 baseball season began, but life back home in their Rochester suburb was not as enchanted as their time in Iowa. The magic of Dyersville could not be packed along with the wedding photos and souvenirs that were brought back to Rochester. The honeymoon ended and the banality of making ends meet, dealing with a family that included five children from previous marriages, and living together took their toll. The Field of Dreams, however, had more magic in its corn for the Ryans.

Five years removed from the wedding at home plate, the couple returned to Iowa at the request of the *Dreamfield* filmmakers who wanted to record their story. Their return to Iowa was like a return to the start of their marriage itself. "When we were feeling back home a lull, a low tide in the relationship with a lot of the stresses of raising a blended family, the call came from Iowa and it said, 'Come back to us,'" Lynn recounted.

Saluted with a place of honor in a Labor Day parade and fed by the memories that met them at every corner of the tiny town, everything seemed right again. "Boy, did we need it," said Lynn. "When we arrived here, we walked right over to home plate and gave each other an anniversary kiss, and you could feel it all coming back—just the boost that we needed for our love." Comforted by the peculiar power of the Field, the Ryans headed back to Rochester armed with a second chance.

Some might subject the field's draw to rigorous analysis, but to Jerry, it is really quite simple. "It was just like all of a sudden you realize that you have to go down to the store to get some milk," he said. "I just realized that for me, this next step of my life, this next stage of my life, I needed to go to the Field of Dreams. That's where I needed to go. It was very simple."

In an original poem Jerry Ryan described the field as follows:

A kind of strange place
That encourages placement of faith
In the kindness of strangers.
Where Lynn and I learned that
The first steps out of purgatory
Turn promises of provision into time
By providing diamond time for promises.

Now, the film *Field of Dreams* and memories of their visits to Dyersville help the Ryans through rough spots in their marriage and keep them focused on what is truly important in life. Their story has been profiled in local and national media, and Jerry and Lynn have discussed their connection to the Field of Dream with both W. P. Kinsella and Phil Alden Robinson.

A schoolteacher, Jerry Ryan uses a bit of the magic to inspire his students. At the end of each school year, Jerry tells his students about his association with the Field of Dreams. He relates his tale in a narrative, shows videos of the wedding and the Ryans' subsequent media coverage, and then gives his class something tangible to take with them. To conclude his end-of-year address, Jerry gives each of his students a little bit of dirt from the Field of Dreams for good luck. Of the token gesture, Jerry states simply, "It's part of my spiritual wealth. It's a little gift that I can give to people that is powerful."

IT'S PERFECT

In *Field of Dreams*, after finally getting to see the magical baseball field and meet "Shoeless" Joe Jackson, Terence Mann looks at the scene and comments, "Unbelievable."

Watching the ballplayers, Ray Kinsella responds, "It's more than that. It's perfect."

The Field of Dreams can be perfect because it is uncomplicated. At its essence it is something simple, just grass and dirt organized as a baseball field with the barest of bleachers and backstop adorning the diamond. That's it. There is no geyser that erupts every minute or an elaborate changing of the guard that occurs every day at noon to entertain tourists. There is no organized game to watch, no exploding scoreboard to lead cheers, and no mascot to entertain children or enthrall fans. There is no monorail around the grounds, no multilingual audio tour to expound on points of interest, and no visitor acclimation center to offer a welcome. It is just a well-kept baseball diamond in the midst of scenic farmland near a peaceful town in the heart of America.

Without its link to the film, the baseball field in the corn is handsome, but most professional diamonds are even more striking—plus they host high-level sports entertainment. Without the field, the Lansing and Ameskamp land is picturesque, but no more so than thousands of other farms. Without its movie set attraction, Dyersville is alluring, but not enough to warrant the tourist traffic that the Field of Dreams creates. But together, the field, connected as it is as a vestige of the film and existing in such a cloistered and bucolic setting, has an appeal as something simple and unspoiled in this overly complicated and oft-corrupted world.

In *Field of Dreams*, the character Terence Mann tells all who will listen that one of the lures of the Field of Dreams will be its ability to connect people to a simpler time. "They'll arrive at your door as innocent as children, longing for the past," he said.

In *Shoeless Joe*, the J. D. Salinger character declares, "They'll turn up your driveway, not knowing for sure why they're doing it, and arrive at your door, innocent as children, longing for the gentility of the past, for home-canned preserves, ice cream made in a wooden freezer, gingham dresses, and black-and-silver stoves with high warming ovens and cast-iron reservoirs."

In a world of instant gratification, the simplicity of a small baseball field in a rural town has appealed to visitors for its ability to release stress and restore visitors' souls. In Dyersville, without traffic, deadlines, or the menacing realities of everyday life to distract them, the people who make the trip can focus on reminiscences of a simpler time.

In Dyersville, life is about hard work and simple pleasures. The rural life is a comfortable, unharried life. Without a deluge of choices for entertainment options, restaurant choices, or major controversies, there is less to worry about, and one can enjoy family and the land in peace. Dyersville is simple, uncomplicated America. Doors and windows are left unlocked, evening quiet is broken only by the twitter of insects, and townsfolk turn out in numbers for high school baseball games.

As if transported to another world, visitors are delivered to a place where memories—from going to a first baseball game with Dad, to eating Grandma's homemade pies warm from the oven, to the smell of Grandpa's aftershave, to lying in the grass with a high school sweetheart—can refresh the soul. The Field of Dreams has become a special place where time has slowed enough for people to be able to catch their breath, think of the past, and remember what truly matters to them.

Maybe that fascination has something to do with Iowa itself. "There is absolutely no way this film could have been made in Los Angeles," said Iowa Film Office manager Wendol Jarvis. "The land in Iowa was a performer just like any actor. The environment is the key to telling the tale—a tale of dreams."

BEAUTIFUL LAND

The word *Iowa* is possibly derived from a Native American word meaning "beautiful land." It is apt, for Iowa is nothing if not beautiful. The state's rolling hills and rich soils create lush and scenic vistas that stretch for miles. From the southeast, where Iowa borders Illinois and Missouri and the Mississippi River cuts through the plains, the state rises gently to the northwest and the South Dakota and Minnesota state lines. With 90 percent of the state's acreage devoted to farming, Iowa is mile after mile of vast open space and fruitful soil.

Much of Iowa's original settlement pattern consisted of quarter sections of 160 acres, with most major thoroughfares running neatly from north to south or east to west. The resulting squares and rectangles of crops in the countryside and horizontal gable-roofed Prairie-style houses in the towns create a pleasing regularity that intensifies the land's rolling vastness. With Iowa rising from its lowest point to its highest point a total of less than a quarter of a mile, across the state's width of more than three hundred miles, that vastness stretches out like a newly made bedspread across the prairie plains.

W. P. Kinsella certainly found something special in Iowa. Although the Canadian-born author grew up on a farm in rural Alberta, he came to Iowa in 1976 to study at the Iowa Writers' Workshop. Iowa was nothing if not inspirational, and the state and its sites figure prominently, almost like another character, in many of his stories. He mentions the larger-than-life black statue of an angel that overlooks an Iowa City grave in *Shoeless Joe* along with the legend that the statue will turn white if a man kisses a virgin at midnight beneath it. The statue actually comes to life and plays the outfield in Kinsella's *The Iowa Baseball Confederacy*. Iowa City's Pearson's drug store and its old-fashioned malts are described as "right out of a Norman Rockwell painting" in *Shoeless Joe*.

Perhaps Iowa just creates a tug, like a caught thread, gently pulling despite attempts to move away. For years, Kinsella and his wife returned to a home they owned in Iowa City where the couple would summer while performing research for upcoming works at the nearby university library.

In *Shoeless Joe*, Ray Kinsella declares, "I knew I loved Iowa as much as a man could love a piece of earth."

Smitten with the Iowa land, author Kinsella concurred. "I fell in love with Iowa City. It's the only place I really feel comfortable." In the introduction to his collection of baseball short stories, *The Thrill of the Grass* (1984), Kinsella describes himself as "a middle-aged writer who likes to stare at the ocean or the Iowa corn fields while I create works of imagination."

James Earl Jones understands the attractiveness fertile farmland and the near-mystical attraction of a cornfield. "I'm a farmer from Michigan, and I know about cornfields," he said, "and what I know about the Iowa cornfields is they're so vast that children get lost in them every year and die because helicopters can't spot them." Jones spoke ominously. "The edge of a cornfield is a great barrier that you can't see through. If you wanted to conjure up a natural phenomenon that is a spiritual barrier as well, then the cornfield is ideal."

SOMETHING FOR EVERYONE

As described in a tourist brochure, the Field of Dreams "exudes everything that is wonderful, the relaxed pace, the pastoral setting, the rich history. The best thing about this place is what isn't here—instead of providing images and dreams, it is content to be a mere stage. It falls to each individual guest to supply whatever drama and whatever cast he or she desires."

For some, it is enough to enjoy the Field of Dreams as a quiet place where people can use their memories and fantasies to sweep them away with emotions or create a connection with a favorite film. One reason visitors to the Field of Dreams have such an opportunity to concentrate is the peacefulness that prevails at the scene. This tranquility creates an atmosphere that encourages quiet reflection and focuses visitors on the experience of the site itself. Others, however, require additional interpretation like the Ghost Players to enjoy the experience. Still others would prefer to host festivals and private gatherings and use the site to generate worldwide attention for Dyersville.

So while some would love to play formal baseball games complete with umpires and crowds on the field, or act in a *Field of Dreams* screen test in the Lansing house, the vast majority of visitors to the Field of Dreams simply join in or enjoy watching the informal pickup games.

The field remains as it was in the film: a baseball diamond in a corn-field. For most visitors, this is exactly as they would have it.

Dreamfield executive producer Tim Crescenti is now a seasoned Field of Dreams batting practice pitcher veteran. During the past de-cade, he has been a regular visitor. On most visits, he unpacks a bag of old baseballs, browned and grass-stained from use, and plants himself on the mound where he will pitch to strangers until the pain in his shoulder makes him step off the diamond. Later, as he struggles to lift his toothbrush before bed, the sore arm is an achy reminder of the simple pleasure he derives from his time on the Field of Dreams—for Crescenti, a comfortable place in a tumultuous world.

Crescenti first visited the field in 1993. Stepping up to the plate, Crescenti was thrilled to knock a fat pitch into the corn. After playing all day, he and his fellow travelers decided they could not let their ex-perience end there. A group of strangers just hours before, the bunch ended their day by renting a VCR and *Field of Dreams* and gathering in Crescenti's hotel room for a viewing.

Amazed at how people opened up to each other at the field, Cres-centi hatched the idea for his *Dreamfield* documentary and labored to complete the project. But the effort turned out to be more than just a professional success. For Crescenti, the former movie set and work site had become a centering and grounding place.

"I go there every single year at least once," he said more than a decade after the first visitor arrived at the Lansing farm. "And last year we went through a stage where my father died, my wife's grand-mother—whom she was close to—died, an uncle died, a very good friend died, all within about ten days, and I was just in a daze. I was in an absolute fog. A month later, Colleen [Crescenti's wife] figured out that I needed to go to the Field of Dreams, and this, of course, was in February, which is not the best time of the year for throwing a baseball around. So my daughter and I went to the field and kind of just walked out to the field in the snow and said our prayers, and it was great."

Even though his career now takes him to exotic locations across the globe, when he finds himself feeling run down by the world and needing to reinvigorate himself, Crescenti finds time to take the trip to Dyersville—bag full of old baseballs in tow. If visitors encounter a tall, dark-haired man who could pass for a sportscaster or an actor, walking around with a sack full of baseballs and a right arm that looks like it might be hanging a little lower than his left, chances are it is Tim.

Without any official organizing mechanism, visitors to the Field of Dreams are left to make their own experiences. Some arrive in twos or pair up to have a catch. Some try to focus young children on learning baseball skills. Those who do not have a desire to play baseball seem to yearn to do something to acknowledge their visit, and so they walk the bases and pose for photographs. Anyone wishing to get in on a catch or take an at-bat is instantly welcomed and anyone volunteering to throw batting practice finds a line of would-be batters who will step up to the plate, one after another, as long as the pitched balls continue to cross the plate as strikes.

Having observed the field and its visitors for more than a decade, Al Ameskamp commented that the field is "a bunch of strangers playing together like they'd known each other all their lives. That's just the way it works out here from morning to night."

Frolicking on the field, people wait their turn to step up to bat and take as many swings as they desire before running back onto the diamond to chase balls. There are no arguments about whose turn it is or how many balls each batter has received. Instead, one hears, "I haven't swung a baseball bat in twenty years," or "Put it here so I can knock one into the corn." Young kids ask pitchers to "Aim it at the bat" as their fathers yell encouraging tips from the outfield. The young at heart confess, "I'll be feeling this tomorrow," but insist on taking full swings at the plate and bending to pick up ground balls.

The games are neither limited to the athletic nor discriminatory toward the infirm. Anyone who is willing to step onto the diamond is invited to participate, and—without any formal guidelines or requirements—players offer any assistance they might require.

This appeal has created a special bond between the Field of Dreams and Camp Courageous of Iowa. The camp, less than a half-hour drive south of Dyersville near Monticello, is a year-round recreational and respite care retreat for people with disabilities. As part of their week or weekend stay, campers climb trees and enjoy farming and canoe. In general, they are challenged to try activities that their limitations usually preclude. "We're always looking for things that we can do with our program here to make it the most challenging, the most rewarding, and the safest possible experience that a camper can have," explained Camp Courageous associate executive director Mike Fortman. "At some point somebody suggested, 'Let's take a group of campers over to the Field of Dreams.'"

In recent years, Camp Courageous has taken a few buses full of about seventy-five campers, mostly youths, up the road to Dyersville to join in on the fun. "It's kind of like opening up the candy shop," Fortman said. "Campers look around, and there's definitely a reaction by the campers when they finally see the Field of Dreams."

But the special visitors don't just get to look at the field. They are encouraged to join in with other visitors as they wander in and out of the corn, have a catch, or step up to the plate. While none of the other visitors are specially prepared for the youngsters from Camp Courageous, they inevitably end up interacting with the campers. "Initially there's some tentativeness, but I think that what the Field of Dreams does is it brings all people together," Fortman remarked. "You get out there on that playing field, and it doesn't matter who's out there with you—all of a sudden they're your teammates. I think that that tentativeness is quickly erased just by the aura of the Field of Dreams."

SOMETHING UNEXPECTED

For Stacy Brannan, a visit to the Field of Dreams was a pleasant surprise. In July 1993, Stacy was home from college for the summer and living with her parents in Knoxville, Illinois. Stacy's mother decided

This composite image helped attract Hollywood to Dyersville, Iowa. Filmmakers were looking for a simple family farm with a flat area for the baseball field near the farmhouse but also wanted the house to be up on a little rise to be more photographically interesting. (Photo courtesy of Wendol Jarvis.)

The Lansing farmhouse awaits it transformation into the Kinsella family home for *Field of Dreams*. Before filming, the house would receive a fresh coat of white paint, a white picket fence, new bay windows, and the now-famous wraparound porch and its porch swing. (Photo courtesy of Wendol Jarvis.)

Location scouts armed with a cover from W. P. Kinsella's *Shoeless Joe*, which featured a view of a white farmhouse next to a red barn in a sea of corn, found the Lansing property ideally suited to bring the book to life. (Photo courtesy of Wendol Jarvis.)

Field of Dreams director Phil Robinson discovers the setting for his film to bring to life the vision W. P. Kinsella created in *Shoeless Joe*. *Field of Dreams* would receive mixed reviews, but hit a homerun with viewers who extended their connection to the film by trekking to the Dyersville movie set. (Photo courtesy of Wendol Jarvis.)

Downtown Dyersville is charming, highlighted by the Basilica of St. Francis Xavier in the distance. Dyersville was better known as the Farm Toy Capital of the World before *Field of Dreams* gave the town new fame. (Photo courtesy of the Dyersville Area Chamber of Commerce .)

The Lansing family (mother Bernice with Mary Lou, Betty, Carol, and Don) on the porch swing overlooking the Field of Dreams. The house had been in the Lansing family for more than eighty years before it found movie stardom. (Photo courtesy of Don and Becky Lansing.)

Becky and Don Lansing. Visitors inspired by the film came to Don's farm. When Becky was inspired by her dream to travel to Iowa, romance blossomed, and marriage followed. (Photo courtesy of Don and Becky Lansing.)

Al and Rita Ameskamp (right). The affable couple signing autographs and interacting with visitors to Left and Center Field of Dreams. Playing host came naturally to the Ameskamps. (Photo courtesy of Al and Rita Ameskamp.)

The Field of Dreams in 1989 with rows of corn in left and center field. Al Ameskamp planted corn on his land following the filming in the summer of 1988 but restored the complete Field of Dreams for visitors the following season. (Photo courtesy of Lynn and Jerry Ryan.)

Lynn and Jerry Ryan pose for a wedding picture at the Field of Dreams after exchanging vows at home plate. The couple came to Iowa looking for a special place to marry and returned years later to recapture the magic. (Photo courtesy of Lynn and Jerry Ryan.)

The Ryan wedding on the Field of Dreams in 1989 was celebrated with rows of corn in left and center field. Dyersville hospitality made the wedding an affair to remember. (Photo courtesy of Lynn and Jerry Ryan.)

Dreamfield executive producer Tim Crescenti preparing to throw batting practice—or take notes—at the Field of Dreams. The film site has provided Crescenti with a pleasant diversion, professional inspiration, and a measure of comfort in his life. (Photo courtesy of Tim Crescenti.)

Shirley Eack disappearing into the corn on a 2000 visit to Dyersville shortly before she passed away. The Field of Dreams is more than a simple tourist attraction for visitors who come seeking personal fulfillment, redemption, or a connection to lost loved ones. (Photo courtesy of Stacy Eack.)

Iowa farmer and team catcher Marv Maiers clowning with a young visitor during an appearance by the Ghost Players at the Field of Dreams. Maiers and his teammates put on an entertaining presentation billed as the "Greatest Show on Dirt." (Photo courtesy of Keith Rahe/Ghost Players.)

The Ghost Players emerge from the Iowa corn to give a taste of Hollywood's vision to Field of Dreams visitors. The Ghost Players—fully clad in authentic reproductions of 1919 Chicago White Sox uniforms—include a state representative, a college baseball coach, and several players who appeared in the film *Field of Dreams* as ballplayers. (Photo courtesy of Keith Rahe/Ghost Players.)

"People will come," declared Terrence Mann in *Field of Dreams*. As if continuing the pilgrimage to the Field of Dreams seen at the end of the film, visitors continue to arrive at the Dyersville former movie set. (Photo courtesy of Wendol Jarvis.)

Young and old, able and challenged join in a loosely organized pick-up game that runs as long as people are willing to play. People from across the globe have found their way to this diamond to race around the bases, shag fly balls, knock one out of the park, and connect with something missing in their lives. (Photo courtesy of Wendol Jarvis.)

Team of Dreams 2019. (Field of Dreams Movie Site Images used with the permission of Go the Distance Baseball LLC.)

that the family should make the four-hour trip to Dyersville. They had seen the film and enjoyed the story and its message, but Stacy's family was not much into baseball. Stacy said that her mother "just wanted to see the corn."

So twenty-nine-year-old Stacy and her parents, Dean and Shirley Eack, who were sixty-seven and sixty-four at the time, packed into the car and made the trip. The journey was not necessarily a spiritual quest or a reverent expedition; it was just an outing for three people looking for something to do with a day, curious about what they would find.

Once they arrived at the field, Stacy found her first pleasant surprise. In the small gravel parking lot, she got out of the car and walked toward the field with her mother when she noticed that her father lagged behind. He was rummaging in the trunk, emerging with a pair of items Stacy found very out of character. "Gosh darn it," she burst out, "he had packed a ball and glove."

Neither Stacy nor her mother were sure that Dean even owned a glove or ball, but there he was, headed out to left field to join the activities. Stacy and Shirley sat in the bleachers with their mouths agape as they watched the suddenly young-at-heart senior citizen join in the pickup game.

Dean had been a baseball fan as a young boy, but he hadn't played in decades. Of her father's unprecedented adventure on the ballfield, Stacy suggested, "He knew it was a safe place to let your hair down." It was a memorable moment.

"I had never seen that side of my dad," Stacy said, mesmerized as she watched a man she only knew as a father suddenly transform into an aged kid playing with the others on the field.

As her father romped in the grass, her mother announced that she was going into the corn. As she watched her mother disappear into the stalks, Stacy confessed that she "halfway expected something to happen." Gazing into the infinite green of a field of mature corn, it is easy to imagine that the panorama of the unknown is truly a gateway to something otherworldly.

Stacy and her parents left Dyersville with a few vials of dirt as souvenirs, photographs of the family at the field, and some poignant memories. The day trip was just to the Field of Dreams and back home, about eight hours of driving for a short time at the destination. The drive back home was quiet, and there was very little talk as each reflected on what Stacy called a "very moving place to go see."

Stacy described her father as "a deep well," not someone who is very expressive with his feelings. At play on the Field of Dreams he showed Stacy a different side of himself. He explained his desire to dust off his old glove and join the participants in the fun as serendipitous. "I thought I may as well play," he said.

But Stacy's mother was more profoundly affected. When she heard about ongoing discussions in Dyersville about whether to permit additional tourist-related activities near the Field of Dreams, she was moved to write a letter about how she thought the field was a particularly special place that should be preserved as is. Don and Becky Lansing were moved to tears by the letter and telephoned Shirley Eack. Shirley was delighted. "It's the lady from the Field of Dreams on the phone," she yelled to her husband.

The Lansings invited Shirley to return to the field and to sit in their porch swing and enjoy their view of the unique venue. Shirley replied that she was getting on in years and that she doubted she would ever be back but warned the Lansings to keep an eye out for her in the corn.

At the field, Stacy was able to gain some perspective on her time with her parents. "I think I knew that [my mom's] years were drawing to a close, so it was kind of a bittersweet kind of day." But seeing her father reveling in the outfield and watching her mother's enthusiasm about her journey into the corn made the day a special trip.

Back home, with her mother struggling with cancer, Stacy suggested a return trip to the Field of Dreams as a way to take the family's collective mind off of the toll that Shirley's disease was taking on them all.

"Let's go back as a family," Stacy prompted.

But her mother replied, "I can't go back in this life."

Shirley Eack died in June 2000, seven years after her trip to Dyersville. Stacy and her father both cherish the photograph of Shirley walking into the corn at the Field of Dreams. When she peered into the corn at the Field of Dreams, Stacy wondered whether something magical waited in the lush rows of leafy stalks. Now she thinks about returning to Dyersville without her parents, but her mother would not be far from her mind. "I'm going to dip into that corn trying to get a glimpse of her," she promised.

Neither a baseball lover nor a movie buff, Stacy was moved by what the field stirred within her. "The world is so mixed up and busy," she said. "It's a simple place. Baseball doesn't change. It reminds you of a simpler time—reminds you how life can be so much simpler."

TURNING BACK THE CLOCK

While the field certainly generates worldwide attention, it even delights many locals. *Wall Street Journal* staff reporter Thomas King was born and raised in Cedar Rapids, Iowa. Taking note of the fact that Hollywood came to Iowa to film both *Field of Dreams* and *The Bridges of Madison County*, King wrote in a 1995 article, "It is no coincidence that Hollywood came to Iowa to make movies about idealism and fantasy. The Iowa locations show off what is arguably the best part of show-biz, the side that helps people let go, dream and be full of hope. That may sound corny, but hey, this is Iowa."

While he may find Hollywood's fascination with the Hawkeye State corny and while he may cast a cynical reporter's eye to the world, King promptly confessed that his own father proposed that the family of seven adults and eight children travel to the Field of Dreams. King's mother thought the setting would be the perfect spot for the family Christmas card photograph. Even native Iowans find the simple charms hard to resist.

In his review of *Field of Dreams* for *Commonweal*, Tom O'Brien declared, "The great strength of *Field of Dreams* is its lack of embarrassment over big things. The real theme of the film isn't baseball, or America, but sunny summer days spent with loved ones at some ideal house, a pathetic but oh-so-human imagination of heaven."

As the catcher for the Ghost Players and the team's clown prince and ringleader, Iowa farmer Marv Maiers is recognizable for his bushy mustache and easy wit. During his performances, Maiers is able to transfer his enthusiasm and sense of fun to shy kids and jaded adults alike. He sees much of the allure of the field in a similar ability to transmit its tranquility to those who visit. "When you come out here—when you park your car over in the lot and you walk over here—whatever was bugging you when you got out of your car, you forget about it," he said. "It's just one little corner of serenity. Everybody seems to need that little cavern you can crawl in and forget about your worries."

With a mythic quality—unfettered by the boundaries of space and time—baseball can transcend the ordinary world to take on legendary proportions. It is possible to conceive of the rally that never ends or the home run that never lands. Baseball fans can then be comforted that the world can be as it was and that any intrusions of changing times can be dismissed as inconsequential to the world within the foul lines and in the lives of those who follow the game. Baseball proceeds at its own unhurried schedule, out by out, season by season, without the ticking of a clock to pressure the pace.

San Francisco sportswriter Herb Caen's wry view of this quality was that "[t]he clock doesn't matter in baseball. Time stands still or moves backward. Theoretically, one game could go on forever. Some seem to."

The official and unofficial keepers of the spirit of the game will point out that the game itself has changed little over the years, so it is essentially the same game as it was a century ago. It can therefore be the same game as had been viewed by successive generations despite the intervening years. Of this quality, former baseball commissioner Bowie Kuhn once stated, "I believe in the Rip Van Winkle theory—that a man from 1910 must be able to wake up after being asleep for seventy years, walk into a ballpark and understand baseball perfectly."

For people who would love to halt the hands of time—to enjoy their young children before they become adolescents, to retain youthful vigor before age saps their strength, to ward off mortality so they can enjoy one more season in the sun—the attraction is obvious. If baseball is not changing, they can forget for the duration of nine innings that the world is. If they buy into the fantasy that the game itself is timeless, each new season can turn back the clock.

Baseball's romantic attractiveness is more than its timelessness. The game's association with the land itself speaks to a connection to the earth. As someone who grew up in farmland, actor James Earl Jones knows this connection and, while making *Field of Dreams*, understood that his movie set was something unique. "There's nothing 'just a movie site' about a farmland like that. It's always something special and, if you want to say, if not sacred, certainly special."

Baseball perpetuates its version of agrarian myth, that the game was raised from the great American countryside, grown from rich farmland to nourish a hungering nation. Baseball's Hall of Fame can be found in Cooperstown, New York, where, legend has it, future Civil War general Abner Doubleday created the game of baseball in a local field. This version of history was given credence by a 1907 commission charged with determining the origin of baseball. The more likely truth, however, is that baseball probably simply evolved over time from a number of games in places where one can assemble at least eighteen individuals to form two baseball teams—cities and towns. In fact, many scholars locate baseball's genesis in less bucolic Hoboken, New Jersey. Baseball would have a very different conception story and resulting historical presentation if its origins traced to an industrial municipality in the shadow of New York City's skyscrapers instead of an agrarian village on Lake Glimmerglass.

A PLACE FOR DREAMERS

Each year, more than a half million visitors bedecked in team colors travel to baseball's shrine in Cooperstown to gaze at the artifacts of the game, revel in the stories of baseball legend, and purchase baseball memorabilia. Visitors to Dyersville are less likely to be clothed in team regalia or searching for collector's items. Baseball definitely contributes to the field's attraction, but the allure goes beyond any game.

In *Cooperstown to Dyersville*, Charles Fruehling Springwood quotes Ron Eberhard, a frequent Field of Dreams visitor and motivational speaker who often talks of the field in his presentations, on the distinction between the two attractions. "People do not come to Dyersville and the 'Field of Dreams' for even close to similar reasons as the 'Baseball Hall of Fame,'" he notes. "The 'Field' is for dreamers and visionaries. Cooperstown is for hero worshippers and those who want to live in the past." The comparison is not set up to be an either/or choice, but as a result of the difference in the attractions, fans of the game visit the Hall of Fame to connect with the game of baseball and its great players and moments. Fans of *Field of Dreams* visit Dyersville to connect with emotions inspired by the film.

Of course, baseball is not an afterthought at the Field of Dreams or in the book and film that inspired it. W. P. Kinsella described his baseball writings as something more than stories about the national pastime. "I am someone who writes peripherally about baseball," he offered. "I agree that the best sports literature isn't really about sports. I, for instance, write love stories that have baseball as a background."

That said, he adamantly declared that his *Shoeless Joe* and the resulting *Field of Dreams* are not about baseball. Of the film, Kinsella stated, "It's not a baseball movie. It's a love story about following dreams and making them come true. Because it's a fantasy about a perfect world, it has to involve baseball, because baseball would have a part to play in a perfect world."

Kinsella said that "*Shoeless Joe* is a novel about a perfect world. It's about a man who has a perfect wife, a perfect daughter, and wants to keep it that way. In a perfect world, you would be able to resurrect the dead. In a perfect world, you could play ball at midnight on the grass of your favorite ballpark."

As the tangible remains of Kinsella's idea and Phil Alden Robinson's interpretation of that vision, the Field of Dreams maintains that attraction for those who would seek a perfect world. With its connection to the national pastime, simple Americana, and the land itself, the Field of Dreams recalls a popular sport, the comfort of another age, and an instinctual attachment to the earth and its bounty.

4

Seeking the Sacred in a Pop Culture World

"And is there enough magic out there in the moonlight to make this dream come true?"

—*Archibald "Moonlight" Graham*

Minister Terry Rush of the Memorial Drive Church of Christ in Tulsa, Oklahoma, declared of the Field of Dreams, "This is the corn cathedral." Rush had a special vantage point from which to make his declaration, for he truly delivered the "Sermon on the Mound."

Rush grew up in Memphis, Missouri, near the Iowa border with aspirations of becoming a major leaguer. He became a minister instead. Alongside religious tomes and scripture, the shelves of Minister Rush's office are stocked with baseball memorabilia. Looking more like a room from the Baseball Hall of Fame than a rectory, the office is piled high with baseballs and gloves, St. Louis Cardinals merchandise, and collector's items from the Field of Dreams. But becoming a minister did not mean that Rush was just relegated to fandom; he remained a player. Rush was a veteran of more than two dozen baseball fantasy camps, playing with and against former major leaguers, when he was invited to attend a special fantasy camp held at the Field of Dreams in September 1992. On the Sunday morning of the camp's weekend, Rush traded in his usual catching gear and took to the mound dressed in a 1919 Chicago White Sox uniform to conduct a worship service.

"I stood on a very special mound at the Field of Dreams, and I delivered something that was different than a baseball," Rush recalled. "I delivered a sermon to a group of people who were gathered for a special worship service on the Field of Dreams. And we delivered a message that was incredible. It was so full of hope. It was so appropriate on this field where it calls, by its very name, people to dream, and that's the entire message of God."

When the sermon began at 8:00 A.M., only a handful of congregants were on hand. But Rush had to stop his talk to allow for fashionably late arrivals as a line of cars appeared on the narrow road leading to the field. To Rush, the parade of vehicles in a line slowly winding up the gravel road "was just like the end of the movie." He was soon playing to a true crowd. One description of the event counted about three hundred people clustered on wet bleachers on the damp morning to receive Rush's message.

Rush's audience consisted of fantasy camp attendees who wanted to hear what their catcher had to say about something other than pitch selection and locals who had seen the special service advertised in local papers. His sermon, using baseball as a metaphor, spoke of becoming a better person and talked of the sacrifice—Christ's death on the cross, not the bunt to move the runner.

To conclude his message to the intimate congregation, Rush declared, "The day would come when there would be a crack and a roar and a shout." But the minister was not talking about baseball and a game-winning home run. He was talking about Armageddon, the end of world. On judgment day, Rush avowed, people would turn the oft-repeated movie phrase on its head and ask, "Is this Iowa?" only to hear, "No, it's heaven."

Some may wonder whether such a religious message should not be delivered in a more traditionally religious place such as Dyersville's gothic Basilica instead of the baseball diamond in a cornfield. By design, houses of worship are built to inspire a sense of the wonder of divine presence. But Terry Rush's message was delivered not in a church but on a former movie set in rural America, affirming the notion that the sacred surely can be found in places that are not traditionally thought of as religious sites.

"There's something about humanity, that we sense an authenticity," Rush said in describing the ability to see the spiritual in everyday life. "We don't know how to describe it, but we know it when we're near it."

People see the divine in nature or sense the divine watching their children grow. Some find spirituality in nature or technology. Some find it in the message of a song, a work of literature, or a piece of art. Some find it in popular culture. "People love to hear of an illustration that is real rather than one constructed from the mind," said Rush.

In a similar manner, Rush saw the spiritual in the combination of natural beauty and human construction that is the Field of Dreams. "The thing that that field says to me is that God really did create that place," Rush said. "It has his touch to it, his design."

When he first saw the Field of Dreams, Rush "couldn't believe that there could be something like that still in America that you could actually just walk on; there were no barriers, no fees."

He marveled, "It's just sitting out there away from everything that is distracting, and it is so simple and so pure, and that's how I see God working in our lives that we clutter it and distract it and try to recover it."

According to the orator of the Sermon on the Mound, the Field of Dreams has generated a numinous appeal independent of its pop culture origin. Of the field's visitors, Rush said, "The movie motivates them, but the field itself is a genuine mystery to the inner person. It's weird. It's wonderfully weird.

"I don't think there's anything ultra- or super- or supraspiritual except the wonder that is contained in a person's heart as would be anything that is simply beautiful."

Despite any rational reason why people visit the Field of Dreams, many visitors cannot put into words why they just had to make the trip. Whether inspired by a dream, like Becky Lansing (formerly DuBuisson), or moved by the site's peaceful simplicity, like Jerry and Lynn Ryan, many visitors to the field freely admit that they do not totally understand the allure. Some even suggest that something special was always lying fallow on the Lansing and Ameskamp land just waiting for the world to discover it; that W. P. Kinsella was preordained to conceive the idea and Hollywood had no choice but to find Dyersville as the place to transform Kinsella's vision into film.

SACRED AND PROFANE

In *The Sacred and the Profane*, religious historian Mircea Eliade explains that the history of religions is constituted by a great number of occasions when something shows itself as sacred. Eliade writes that the sanctified can present itself as something wholly other than the secular even if it is manifested in an object or place that is otherwise unremarkable. Thus, in an apparent paradox, a tree or a mountain may appear as any other tree or mountain to most, but for those to whom the objects have revealed themselves to be sacred, the tree or mountain reaches a higher reality. Thus, what is sacred is not limited to that which could be traditionally construed as connected to religion.

Thinking of existence would indeed seem dull if people believed that life consisted of their daily routines alone. But thinking that life has a greater cosmic purpose is a reassuring notion. The faithful will, therefore, travel from across the globe to bask in the holy glow of a place where they believe they can find the spiritual—for it is there that they can be reawakened to the notion that there is more to life than the profane.

The town of Lourdes in southwestern France attracts five million visitors each year who travel to a site where, in 1858, a teenage girl named Bernadette saw a vision of a white-robed lady in a grotto. According to believers, Bernadette discovered a spring in the grotto that is reputed to have miraculous healing powers. Places like Lourdes, held as sacred by the faithful, attract scores of pilgrims who believe that they can find spiritual fulfillment, miraculous cures, or divine revelation at their destination. Because these destinations are much more than just tourist attractions to those pilgrims (although such sites have many of the accessories that are found at tourist traps), these sites attract throngs of nontraditional tourists. Many visitors will save for a lifetime to make a trip or will travel in the least-luxurious manner to be able to reach their objective. Instead of searching for postcards and trinkets, they may seek hope, religious salvation, or a remedy they cannot find in medical science.

It is a form of self-fulfilling prophesy to declare that pilgrims feel moved when they reach their destination. Of course, they travel to their destinations believing that something spiritual or miraculous may occur at the site, and they arrive with a heightened state of anticipation and awareness. They are ready to believe and experience something special.

Many people expect to find some form of magic in the Iowa corn and therefore arrive at the field with heightened expectations, looking for something miraculous like the events they read about in the book or saw in the film. In this sense, the visitors actually arrive with the magic in their hearts, believing that they may find what they are looking for at the Field of Dreams. Much as after taking a placebo, a patient begins to expect healing to occur, visitors who set out for Dyersville believing that their destination sits on hallowed ground arrive ready to find something spiritual amid the corn.

BASEBALL AND RELIGION

The connection of the Dyersville attraction to the religious makes more sense considering that it is baseball that helps tell the stories in *Shoeless Joe* and *Field of Dreams*. The national pastime's ability to inspire religious devotion is well documented. Given its strong link to the past and insistence that the goings-on in a ballpark are much more significant than just a game, baseball certainly has devotees who are convinced that the national pastime is something more than sport— that it is something holy.

In the book *Shoeless Joe*, Ray Kinsella frets over how he is supposed to ease the pain of J. D. Salinger. Kinsella desperately tries to communicate his passionate feelings for baseball with the reclusive author and sermonizes about a baseball crowd, "We're not just ordinary people, we're a congregation. Baseball is a ceremony, a ritual, as surely as sacrificing a goat beneath a full moon is a ritual. The only difference is that most of us realize that it is a game."

Later in the novel, after the man who claimed to be the oldest living Cub is revealed to be a pretender, he finds a measure of redemption as the enchanted ballfield transforms his false claim into truthfulness. After watching himself take the field as a younger man, he evangelizes about the national pastime. With near-frenzied preaching, he touts the spiritual in the game, causing ghost players and the Kinsella clan to chant the word *baseball*. The sermon winds down with the supplication "Praise the name of baseball. The word will set captives free. The word will open the eyes of the blind. The word will raise the dead."

Former Mets manager Wes Westrum echoed the notion that baseball has an element of religion to it. "Baseball is like church," he said. "Many attend, but few understand." Like much of religion, the essence of the game is often lost even on believers. Some fans will scoff at those claims, but there is definitely something in the game that is identified with the spiritual. True ballplayer chatter includes the reverent praise for a good hitter: "he could hit God's fastball." Characters of the game joke that the Bible itself starts with "In the big inning."

The 1907 song "Brother Noah Gave Out Checks for Rain" tells the story of a Deacon Jones and his idea to hold a baseball game to raise funds to repair his church roof. When questioned by his parishioners whether baseball is an appropriate game for "church folks," Jones replied:

Does not the good book say?
That Eve stole first and Adam second
St. Peter umpired the game
Rebecca went to the well with a pitcher

And Ruth in the field won fame,
Goliath was struck out by David a base hit made on
Abel by Cain,
The Prodigal son made one home run,
Brother Noah gave out checks for rain.

Although some scholars doubt that baseball was first conceived by Abner Doubleday in Cooperstown, even the most devout supporters would stop short of suggesting that the game is divinely ordained. That said, in the film *Bull Durham*, the character Annie Savoy notes that she gave Jesus a chance after hearing that there are 108 beads in a Catholic rosary and 108 stitches in a baseball.

Baseball fields are often referred to as cathedrals, a label rarely associated with basketball arenas, football stadia, or hockey rinks. When lined with chalk and set under a clear blue sky, the baseball field is a manicured surface of neatly trimmed grass and carefully sifted dirt that is playing surface as art. A visitor to a baseball field gravitates naturally to the field's focus: home plate. Hockey fans can skate toward a goal, but which one? Basketball and football fans face the same dilemma. Not baseball fans. Just as a church has a pulpit, the ballpark has home plate. The classic ballpark, large enough to inspire awe but intimate enough to allow fans and players to feel each other's presence, creates an eerie stillness when empty as if the field itself has a kinetic energy. In *Shoeless Joe*, W. P. Kinsella speaks through the fictional Ray Kinsella, declaring, "A ballpark at night is more like a church than a church."

One of the game's most passionate fans and most eloquent advocates, Bartlett Giamatti, concluded "I agree with the argument that sports can be viewed as a kind of popular or debased religion, in the sense that the most intense feelings are brought to bear or in the sense that sports may mirror whatever avowedly 'sacred' concerns Americans do share."

Giamatti stated that "[i]f there is a truly religious quality to sport, then, it lies first in the intensity of devotion brought by the true believer, or fan. And it consists second, and much more so, in the widely shared, binding nature—the creedlike quality—of American sport.

"The point is," he decided, "sport is ceremony wherever you find it. It mimics the ritual quality of religious observances even when sport is no longer, if it ever was, connected to a formal religious act of worship."

Of course, Giamatti recognized a clear distinction between religion, with its deeper moral standing, and sport, with its emphasis on performance. "Whether celebrated by Pindar or Roger Angell, sport is, however, ultimately subversive of religion because while it mimics religion's ritual and induces its fanaticism and sensation, sport cares not at all for religion's moral strictures or political power or endless promises. Sport cares not for religion's *consequences.*"

FAITH AND BELIEF

Americans have strong religious beliefs but do not necessarily have strong ties to organized religion. When asked whether they believed in God, 96 percent of Americans responded affirmatively to a survey conducted by Princeton Survey Research Associates in April 2000. However, as any cleric would confirm, the percentage of Americans who regularly attend religious services is much lower in most communities. So there is belief in something—a higher power, a greater good—and also an ongoing search for where to find that something and how to recognize that significance in a manner of worship.

Many religious doctrines proclaim that geographic locations or physical objects have extraordinary powers that range from the ability to predict the future to the ability to promote fertility. Whether these places or items are actually imbued with power may be debated, but their abilities to channel belief and serve as a conduit for spiritual conviction are well established. The faithful will go to great lengths or travel great distances to come into proximity with the holy or to have contact with what they believe are hallowed relics in the hope that they can facilitate something miraculous in their lives. It is that faith that has true magic and real power, not the objects or the places themselves.

Certainly, that faith can act alone while the object or the site cannot. A believer can experience a transformation through faith, but a nonbeliever cannot experience the same transformation through contact with a physical object reputed to be holy. Convictions, not commodities, have true power.

Individuals do not have to attend religious services to have faith, and people do not have to enter a church to believe in something that the scientific world cannot explain. Thus, if faith may represent belief in something that people cannot otherwise prove to themselves, it should be no surprise that many find ways to reinforce that faith in different places—including the secular world.

In the same April 2000 survey that noted an overwhelming belief in God, results showed that 84 percent of Americans believe that God performs miracles, 79 percent believe that the miracles described in the Bible actually took place, and 48 percent have personally experienced or witnessed what they considered to be a miracle. Additionally, 67 percent of the respondents admitted to having prayed to God or a saint for a miracle, and 20 percent admitted to having prayed at a shrine or holy place where they believed that miracles were performed. The survey apparently did not inquire whether respondents believe that Joe Jackson ever appeared in an Iowa cornfield and never even queried whether the outfielder should be in the Baseball Hall of Fame—but its results suggest that Americans are willing to suspend disbelief to accept what some would label as the impossible.

Vinnie and Nancy Caruso of Madison, Wisconsin, have been frequent visitors to the Field of Dreams. Inspired by stories in the local newspaper of the field and its visitors, the Carusos made their first journey to Dyersville in 1990. From her first visit, Nancy described the site as "heaven on Earth." Having formed an attachment to the former movie site, the Carusos' fond memories of their visits keep them coming back to a place where they find strangers who become friends and even evidence of a higher power.

Vinnie noted how stepping onto the Field of Dreams is like stepping outside the day-to-day world and into another reality. "We're away from society as a whole," he said. "We're in our own utopia."

"There's peace. There's tranquility. Time stops," Nancy added. "You don't have any problems.

"Everybody goes to the field to find a healing of anything that they're carrying. I think anybody tries to go to the field to find their inner peace—that there is a God in this crazy, crazy world. And you can take a moment and hear the corn rustling. I can do that ten minutes, fifteen minutes from our house here in Madison, but it's not the same. This isn't just a cornfield. This is a cornfield that, between Lansing and Ameskamp, they kept. They kept something so simple, almost sacred."

HALLOWED GROUND

Addressing the concept of sanctifying the cemetery at Gettysburg, President Abraham Lincoln considered carefully his ability to help make sacred the ground, declaring, "In a larger sense, we can not dedicate—we can not consecrate—we can not hallow, this ground. The brave men, living and dead, who struggled here, have consecrated it, far above our poor power to add or detract."

Meaning can be derived from significant historical events or from contrived fiction. Many of the visitors to the Field of Dreams talk of the spirituality of the former movie set, moved by their association of the events of the film's fiction with the movie set that remains.

Vicky Maus visited the Field of Dreams in 2000 with a friend and her friend's family, but it was the presence of a departed loved one that made Vicky pause. Although Vicky's mother died three years before her trip, Vicky often felt that her mother was with her in her life. Pausing at the field, Vicky suddenly thought, "You've been here, haven't you?" overcome with the notion that her baseball-loving mother was as close as the corn. Maybe such an occurrence could not pass a scientifically rigorous test to certify the episode as paranormal, but to Vicky, the closeness of her mother was all she needed to feel to believe.

Darrel Christenson traveled with a friend from Rochester, Minnesota, to the Field of Dreams in 1994. Arriving in Dyersville, he had a sense that something was going to happen. "It was like we were going to find something there but didn't know exactly what it was going to be," he said. "I'm not sure how high my expectations were on that, but I just sensed that something was about to happen in my life."

While he was having a catch in the outfield, something did happen. As he walked to retrieve a ball from an errant throw, he felt something. "A little breeze came up and I looked out of the left corner of my eye toward the corn, a little bit more into right field, and I can almost see my grandfather there—who had passed away maybe fifteen years earlier," he said. "And he was standing there in his trousers and shirt and his grayish hair always combed back perfectly, and he was just standing there and kind of smiling, and I had a double take. It was the oddest thing to see him there because I had not been thinking of him that often, and I certainly wasn't thinking of him going to the field in that context at all, but this breeze came up, and my grandpa was there."

Darrel, who had been born without a right arm or sight in his right eye, connected with his past and found a place where he would not have to worry about the challenges he faced. "It was a total feeling of acceptance that everybody was accepted for who they were on that field," he said. "We were just throwing the ball around, and it was almost like in a perfect world where everybody was accepted for who they are with their differences with their abilities with their struggles with their issues with their talents—everything. It was a total package of acceptance there.

"It's life in its purest form. It's down to the wooden bats, it's down to no glitz and glamour like so much of America is right now, and it was life down to its simplest form on the farm at the field—and that, to me, was part of the spiritual experience."

Since most of the people who decide to visit the Field of Dreams—and most adults in general—live in a stage of spiritual understanding where belief in the divine is accepted but actual dogma may be questioned, they are generally willing to believe that spirituality can be found in places not thought of as traditionally related to religion. For many of those moved by the story of the power of dreams and the allure of second chances, both *Shoeless Joe* and *Field of Dreams* have provided not only entertainment but inspiration to seek out a site where they could see whether the themes of the book can be captured in real life.

The notion of a search for something sacred in the secular world is a complement to, not a substitute for, organized religion. No site, however naturally beautiful or dramatically poignant, can go much beyond serving as a trigger or a reminder for concepts or ideals learned from another context. The gently undulating hills of corn surrounding the Field of Dreams can remind people of nature's bounty and their good fortune to be blessed enough to live in a land of plenty. The sights of families having a catch on the special diamond can focus them on the important roles that loved ones play in their lives. The underlying ethics and values that the site inspires must come from a system of ethical beliefs that visitors carry with them to the field. Religious theology or worldly philosophy supply the teachings. The site provides the reminder. All people must do is pay attention and recognize the opportunity.

Searching for Redemption and Reconciliation amid the Corn

"For it is money they have and peace they lack."

—*Terence Mann*

Mark Babiarz was seventeen years old when his high school sweetheart became pregnant with their son. Babiarz and the boy's mother decided against marrying, and it was agreed that he would have no role in raising the child. As his friends worked to earn money for car payments and dates, Babiarz earned money to pay for hospital bills. He helped choose a name for the child but signed legal documents outlining responsibilities during the pregnancy and clarifying that he would have no relationship with the boy.

Babiarz spent many nights wondering whether he had made the right decision. "I think I didn't know which direction I was going to go to, and I know we would have gotten a lot of support if we would have gotten married and did the things that a person is supposed to do," he said. "I don't know if the right decisions were made, but I don't know the right decision would have been to stay together and to raise a boy under the circumstances."

Neither Babiarz nor his family had any role in raising the child. Babiarz's son grew up without his biological father. Babiarz saw the child once at a local grocery store when the boy was an infant, but they never had any contact or any relationship. For more than eighteen years, Babiarz had no son.

After high school graduation, Babiarz moved on with his life—moved on from his life—leaving his hometown in Illinois to move to Florida. A passionate baseball fan, Babiarz enjoyed the Florida sun and the chance to see spring training, minor league games, and—with baseball expansion—major league action. He served in the air force, went to college, married, fathered a daughter, and began a career as a financial consultant. He and his wife eventually divorced, but despite the changes in his personal and professional life, he never forgot the son he never knew.

He often reflected on his life and how a son miles away was growing up without his father in his life. Once, while visiting family back home, curiosity got the best of him, and he drove by his son's house in an unsuccessful attempt to get a glimpse of the boy. "There were many times I sat in bed, and I would just sit there for hours and just think, 'What if this happened or what if that happened?'" he said. "Of course, many tears were shed during that time of uncertainties, and of course all the guilt that was piling on me, knowing what I did was not exactly right, but I made the decision and I had to live with it."

Babiarz thought about reaching out to his son but worried it could cause more problems than it would solve. He reasoned, "It was part of the deal, and I didn't want to interfere with his life. I didn't want to cause any heartaches or situation that would ever complicate his life. I didn't want to do that. His life was complicated enough."

Christopher Albrecht's life was complicated. He grew up wondering who his true father was. Albrecht's grandfather served as a father figure early in his life and his mother eventually married, but there was always something missing for him. By the time he turned eighteen, the curiosity and longing to connect to his roots became too intense. Albrecht—with the support of some in his family, but against the advice of his mother—initiated a series of phone calls to find his father. "It's hard not knowing the other half of the story," he said. "I figured I would go and find him."

Albrecht tracked down Babiarz's sister. She gave Babiarz his son's phone number. On July 5, 1995, Babiarz made the call that would begin to lift the weight of guilt from his shoulders and address all of the questions that nagged Albrecht for a lifetime: "What's your actual dad like? Is he anything like you? How come he's not here?"

Albrecht recalled many times during his youth when he would watch other fathers and sons and wonder why he had to suffer doubts about who he was. He would look around at high school football games and think, "You see all these other friends with their dads, and where's mine?"

Despite support from his family and friends, his inner longing remained, gnawing at his self-esteem. "It's definitely a lonely feeling," he said, confessing to feeling "maybe a little bit of betrayal when you're growing up—how come he's not there?"

Babiarz remembered being fraught with worry wondering why, after all those years, his son was seeking him out. "That day was a very emotional day because I started thinking, 'What in the heck is he calling me for?'" he recalled. "Eighteen years was sitting on that phone number in my hand—all that weight. There was a tremendous boulder that just entered on my shoulders on that day. It was just incredible because it was a point that, when it hit that day, was when I started measuring my life and what I'd accomplished and where I was going in my life."

He wondered about what the boy he never knew wanted. What kind of questions would he have? Would he be angry? Would he want to exact some form of revenge? Would he just want to say hello, or would he want to initiate some kind of relationship?

On the phone, Mark and Chris started off like the strangers they were. In an attempt to better introduce himself, Babiarz —the longtime White Sox fan—told his son about how he and a friend had initiated an effort to get "Shoeless" Joe Jackson enshrined in the Baseball Hall of Fame. Babiarz even printed "Re-Instate 'Shoeless' Joe Jackson" buttons that blare their message in red and white. Chris mentioned that he gave a speech in high school about the Black Sox scandal. They formed a first link.

Though they had never met or even spoken, their lives ran on parallel tracks. They both attended the same high school and were members of the baseball team. They both played third base. Like his father, Albrecht enlisted in the air force after high school.

The conversation was not just about catching up. The newly reunited father and son also talked about what had been missed. Babiarz recalled the words that weighed heaviest on him. "He said, 'I wish you'd been there for my games,'" Babiarz remembered. "And that really hurt me when he said that, and it just put a bunch more rock on my shoulder to carry. That rock got pretty heavy."

But Babiarz was moved by his son's understanding of the painful choice he made. He recalled that Chris—then a little older than his father had been when Chris's mother became pregnant—reflected how he would have responded to the same pressure. Babiarz remembered his son said, "I really don't know what I would have done."

Months before his son reentered his life, Babiarz had become consumed with the concept of reconciliation. But the reconciliation was not for himself. After enduring the 1994 baseball strike, Babiarz and his softball coach, Tom Malone, got the notion that baseball did something wrong in 1994—canceling the World Series due to labor strife—but could begin to make things right by reconciling with the banished Joe Jackson.

When he became involved with the effort to reinstate "Shoeless" Joe Jackson, Babiarz watched the film *Field of Dreams* with new intensity. He found himself thinking not only of reconciliation for baseball and redemption for Joe Jackson but of redemption for himself. As Kevin Costner reunited with his fictional father at the end of the film, Babiarz wondered about his own son. "Would I ever play catch with him? Would it ever happen? Would we ever do that? Would it ever exist?"

After he spoke with his son for the first time, Babiarz could finally begin to think about that redemption and how the pressure he was feeling could be relieved. "When I got off the phone, my life changed," he said. "I had to step back and start weighing everything, and it was like judgment day. It was a self-imposed judgment day."

When they continued their conversation with another phone call, Babiarz told his son that he planned to visit the Field of Dreams while seeing family in Illinois. He extended the invitation to his son. "I said, 'Hey, I'm going to the Field of Dreams. Would you like to meet me there?'"

Chris liked the idea. "He said when he meets me, he wanted to meet me at a significant place," he recalled. "The Field of Dreams sounded like a really neat idea—I was all for that."

While telephone conversations could acquaint the two, Mark and Chris decided to meet for the first time so they could come together face-to-face and begin to answer questions about themselves and each other. They decided to try to move from being curious strangers toward becoming father and son.

Though Babiarz lived in New Port Richey, Florida, and Albrecht was stationed hundreds of miles away in San Antonio, Texas, they would meet for the first time at the former movie site. Dyersville was certainly not a midpoint or even a mutually convenient destination. The Field of Dreams was selected because of what Babiarz and Albrecht believed could be found there—acceptance, belonging, and a place where people believe in second chances. "What struck me about the movie," said Babiarz, "was the scene about playing catch with Dad. People come to this place for reconciliation. Every time I watch that movie, I get a tear in my eye."

The morning of the meeting had started with storms and a powerful downpour, but by the time Babiarz arrived at the field, the day turned bright. Black skies gave way to sunshine and then oppressive heat. He wondered whether the changes in the weather would be a favorable omen. With his parents, sister, nephew, daughter, and future second wife beside him, Babiarz sat on the tiny wooden bleachers. Babiarz—a sturdy, mustachioed man with round glasses, receding brown hair, and a bit of a middle that betrayed the fact he had moved on from competitive baseball to beer league softball—surveyed a field full of fathers and sons and *Field of Dreams* fans. He anxiously examined each car that pulled up, looking for a son he had never met.

"How can you make it up?" he recalled wondering. "There is so much that was missed—that was that rock that I was carrying on my shoulders. I was wondering what in the heck can I do? Will I be able to fulfill anything?"

Babiarz questioned his expectations for the meeting. "The worst thing was that I would never see him again. The worst thing is he'd be angry with me and hate me, and the best thing is having a relationship that would start from that point in his life. . . . Hopefully I can be some part in his life and just to hear him say, 'Hey, Dad,' would be the greatest."

Albrecht, a tall, athletic young man, approached the field with his grandmother, cautiously walking from the parking area toward the baseball diamond and a father he never knew. Like his father, Chris sought a connection to ease the nagging sense of detachment he felt in his life. He remembered thinking, "I expected maybe we could establish a relationship—that's flesh and blood right there. I sure hope I could have a relationship with him."

Just steps from where Kevin Costner's Ray Kinsella reunited with his fictional father, Babiarz and Albrecht shook hands and hugged. After some awkward chit-chat, Babiarz breached the unease by asking, "Got your glove?" Years of uncertainty and anonymity began to fade like ghosts into the corn. Babiarz, Albrecht, and the mixed family posed for photographs, ate a picnic lunch, and shared family pictures and became acquainted.

"I just wanted to know who he was," said Albrecht of his quest to meet his father. For eighteen years neither father nor son had knowledge of each other. At the Field of Dreams, a father seeking redemption and a son searching for reconciliation took gloves and a ball onto the baseball diamond and continued their conversation in the form of a catch.

As the corn rustled with the gentle breeze, Babiarz had a catch with his father, his daughter, and—for the first time—his son. "It was a lot of anticipation," he remembered, "But as we were playing catch, the things were starting to ease and feel more comfortable."

As the father who had never met his son, Babiarz realized that the encounter was more than comfortable. "What happened when we met was, it was a reconciliation," he said.

After their Field of Dreams reunion, Mark and Christopher traveled to Chicago to take in a White Sox game and, with unsteady first steps, began a true familial relationship. It may be impossible to erase eighteen years of emptiness and questions with a few conversations, but the meeting at the field built on a biological bond and established a lasting connection.

"You have to go to the next step," Albrecht said, having resolved some of the issues that had confronted him. "You have to keep going forward—instead of worrying about yesterday. If you thrive on yesterday, you'll never be able to move on."

Five years after meeting his father for the first time, Albrecht contemplated his pending marriage to the mother of a young boy who, much like himself, was growing up without his father. Having endured the questions that went along with a fatherless youth and having filled out an identity by reconnecting with his kin, Albrecht found himself in a unique position to relate to his future stepson. "I just know I have to be there for him," he said. "I definitely have a lot to relate to this guy—the way he started out was pretty much the way I started out."

By connecting with his roots and recovering a portion of an identity he always questioned, Albrecht could help himself and his stepson, but he could not help his father find redemption. On that count, Albrecht was adamant that Babiarz had to find that for himself. "I don't think I can grant it," he said definitively.

Babiarz did find his redemption. "One of the things I think I was able to do with the reconciliation is forgive myself," Babiarz said of the lasting effect of his trip to the Field of Dreams. "Some people could do that in church. Well, we were able to do that right there."

For those who wonder whether reconciliation is possible or whether redemption is real, Babiarz counseled, "Go the distance—you gotta take the risk and take the chance for what's there. If you don't take it, you'll never gain from that experience."

LOOKING FOR FORGIVENESS

Many people long for reconciliation and redemption but lack the tools to achieve reunions or forgiveness, and so they seek surrogates—greeting cards, song lyrics, and lines of poetry. Many of the visitors to the Field of Dreams long for the chance to do what they saw in the movies: get a second chance and make the wrong right.

People say hurtful things. They love those close to them. Unfortunately, the two often intersect in the most extreme ways. They say things they shouldn't. They stubbornly refuse to make amends. They part ways. Over the course of a lifetime, people find an endless array of reasons to feel shame or regret. Unfortunately, that capacity is not always complemented by an ability to apologize or forgive. Once the damage is done, most lack the words, the finesse, or the will to reconcile. They need an event, a catalyst, or an intermediary to make them realize the foolishness of their ways and to encourage them to reestablish severed bonds.

For those who attempt to mend relationships, the Field of Dreams has become a sanctuary. Unable to apologize or express emotions elsewhere in the world, many have come to Dyersville to find the words to say "I'm sorry" and allow feelings to flow freely.

Stories of reconciliation are as old as human history and are interwoven with religious—as well as popular—culture. From the story of Joseph reestablishing a relationship with the brothers who sold him into slavery to Jesus' parable of the prodigal son, reconciliation is exemplified throughout the Bible. From Shakespeare's *King Lear* to Dostoevsky's *Crime and Punishment*, reconciliation plays a central theme throughout classical Western literature. Throughout popular culture, characters long for and find reconciliation. Even Hollywood exhorts entertainment consumers to find a way to forgive and accept to end their suffering. Just as Ray Kinsella is able to mend his relationship with his late father, Luke Skywalker is able to bond with his father Darth Vader at the end of the original *Star Wars* trilogy; Ben and Laura are able to overcome the almost incestuous twists in their relationship to run away together in *The Graduate*; and George Bailey is able to find satisfaction in his existence in *It's a Wonderful Life*.

In song, the Ronettes coo that "the best part of breaking up is when you're making up," Peaches and Herb declare that "we both are so excited 'cause we're reunited," and Paul Simon claims that "the mother and child reunion is only a motion away."

In *Shoeless Joe*, on the eve of his meeting with "Moonlight" Graham, Ray Kinsella notes, "We are mixing a cocktail of memories, and history, and love, and imagination. Now we must wait and see what effect it will have on us."

In life, the words "I am sorry" are often hard to form, and an olive branch is not always handy for the offering. For many visitors, however, the Field of Dreams serves as an ice breaker or vehicle for the reconciliation process. In the film, Ray Kinsella uses the creation of the enchanted baseball diamond and the magic it creates to recall fond memories of his father. Despite the animosity of the past, the process of creating and tending his field is able to undo the hardening of Kinsella's heart so that he is ready for the climactic reconciliation with his father. Real people have used the movie set to create similar connections and enable similar reconciliations. No mere photographic opportunity, this site represents a haven safe from the past and offers an opportunity for visitors to start anew.

In sports, it is always possible to find redemption through on-field performance. After four strikeouts, a batter can win the game with an extra-inning home run and be a hero. After making many mistakes in life, most people do not get to become heroes through a single action.

In sports, redemption can come instantly. In life, redemption takes effort, time, and perseverance.

In an article published in the *Sociology of Sport Journal* titled "Fielding Our Dreams: Rounding Third in Dyersville," Ithaca College professor Stephen Mosher declared that this aspiration transcends mere desire and achieves mythological proportions: "The redemption myth of *Field of Dreams* may be as powerful as the creation myth of Cooperstown that so dominates baseball."

Bartlett Giamatti echoed the thought that sport and redemption can mix. "I believe we cherish as Americans a game wherein freedom and reunion are both possible," he wrote. "Baseball fulfills the promise America made itself to cherish the individual while recognizing the overarching claims of the group."

Thus, people like Mike Babiarz travel to Dyersville to explore that redemption myth and to find out whether they can achieve reconciliation amid the Iowa corn. One of Don Lansing's favorite stories about the visitors to his land involves a father who brought two feuding sons together at the field for a reconciliation. They arrived divided but left speaking to each other. Lansing has watched families come together and has seen grown men kneeling on the field, crying. The reconciliation theme is played out by husbands and wives, fathers and sons, and entire families. They come by the carload, full of trepidation and apprehension. They leave recommitted to each other and without a dry eye.

REDEMPTION AT LAST

Carl Peterson and Phyllis Bethke traveled to the Field of Dreams in search of a form of wholeness. On July 1, 1992, Carl and Phyllis married at the magical field. Their wedding announcement declared that they "were united in marriage at Homeplate on the Field of Dreams." They wore matching Minnesota Twins shirts and celebrated with a cake decorated with a rendering of the Field of Dreams—complete with farmhouse and rows of corn—drawn in gooey icing.

"When you go to the field, there's a feeling of promise of wonderful things yet to come," Phyllis said. "I can remember coming up over that rise. . . . We came over this crest or a little rise of a hill and the lights were on, and I absolutely got goosebumps. It was like a reverence—like a church out in the middle of a cornfield."

Carl also felt goosebumps but never actually saw the field. He had been born almost totally sightless and was totally blind before he graduated from high school. At the Field of Dreams, Carl found acceptance. "Nobody that day said a thing to me about having no vision," he said. "'What are you doing there?'" he said. "I didn't hear it once. I was one of them; they were one of us."

At the Field of Dreams, the games of catch halted to allow for the marriage ceremony, and the ballfield chatter and squeals of joy hushed to allow Carl and Phyllis to recite their vows. They came to the field as individuals and left united in marriage—perhaps the couple used to dealing with the limitations of blindness left feeling more complete.

"I think it's a promise of things to be fulfilled," Phyllis said of the attraction. "I feel that a lot of people look to belong to society or to be one or to be whole and they never achieve it. I think your physical infirmities or attributes don't count for diddily when you go to a place like that. Everyone becomes whole."

The first two words viewers of *Field of Dreams* hear are spoken by Kevin Costner as Ray Kinsella. He begins an introduction to the story just after the primary credits and his first words are "my father." Those are also the first two words of *Shoeless Joe*, although the book and film go in slightly different directions after those words. After the *Field of Dreams* credits roll, the last words that grace the screen before the final fade to black form a dedication "For Our Parents." The simple phrase can be seen as a grand attempt at reconciliation on behalf of all grown children who, mellowed by age and facing the responsibility of parenthood themselves, look for a way to acknowledge their newfound appreciation of their parents' sacrifices and guidance.

Intentional or not, the two phrases bookend the film nicely and frame the idea of wholeness or redemption that the film inspires. In the beginning, a character speaks of his father. In the end, the film is dedicated for parents. First a fictional son discusses his father, then the filmmaker pays tribute to his mother and father. It would be nice to believe that everyone could make the transformation from describing a parent from a distance to embracing parental bonds with acclaim. Perhaps it would be ideal.

The quest for fulfillment extends to people of all abilities and disabilities. W. P. Kinsella views the world created in his novel as a perfect world, and he specifically has noted that part of that perfection is a perfect family. Readers of the book, viewers of the film, and visitors to the Field of Dreams have identified with that view of perfection, and many have responded by aspiring to make their family a happy one.

At the field, many have discovered a vehicle, a conduit, or a vocabulary to mend rent bonds or even find redemption. The perfect world may exist only in novels or on film, but for those who have achieved their reconciliations in Dyersville, the fictional inspiration from *Field of Dreams* and the grass and dirt of the movie site comes very close indeed.

America's Pastime and Its Fathers and Sons

"The one constant through all the years, Ray, has been baseball."

—*Terence Mann*

Kent Nelson grew up in the Denver area as the first-born son of a former marine. Kent and his brother and two sisters formed an active and athletic family, with their father, John, filling roles as their dad at home and their coach on the athletic field. As a grown man, married with two sons of his own and enjoying professional success as a chiropractor in Laramie, Wyoming, Kent saw *Field of Dreams*.

After viewing the tale of father–son reconciliation, Kent sat misty-eyed in the theater as the credits rolled. He was even more moved while reading the book *Shoeless Joe*. But it wasn't until he was flipping through a travel brochure of Midwest attractions that he discovered that the actual movie set field still graced the Lansing and Ameskamp land. Kent decided that he wanted to go see it.

"I didn't know what it was," Kent admitted. "I knew what that movie was, and it was haunting and it was mystical. It was magical, and I just thought, 'If in fact that place still exists, I'd like to go walk around on it and see what it was like.'"

But his idea did not end there. Expanding his vision, Kent thought, "I would like to share that a lot with my father." From that notion, he built the concept into a larger undertaking. He decided to include his younger brother, Kim, and his two sons, Jeff and Robbie.

Kent shared his idea with his wife, who was supportive and pleased with idea but just did not have the emotional attachment to the film that Kent had. Channeling his profound reaction into making a trip to Dyersville work, Kent formed his invitation into a letter asking his father, brother, and sons to be his guests to make a pilgrimage east. Kent recalled that the sentiment from his letter was "I'd like you to be a part of something that I've experienced in a movie setting. I found out that this place actually exists. I'd like to go see it, and you're four of the people in the world that I invite to my special little corner, and let's go see what it's all about."

Kent's sons Jeff and Robbie were a little more skeptical, thinking their dad was a bit crazy for wanting to take them on a journey to see the former movie set. Brother Kim was cool to the idea initially, and Kent's father John was dubious at first. "I think my dad really thought I'd probably lost my mind for a while," said Kent.

That reaction just about sums up his father's thoughts. "I wondered at the moment whether he'd jumped the track or not," John said. "But then as I questioned him and found that he actually was sincere about it, it became a wonderful thing in my mind."

Kent sent his family copies of *Shoeless Joe* and encouraged them to see *Field of Dreams*. John saw the film and enjoyed it a great deal. The crazy idea was turning into something real.

Enthusiasm and persistence finally paid off. The effort took many months to plan, but finally Kent coordinated school and work schedules, cajoled his reluctant relatives to join in on the trip, and arranged all of the logistics for flights, rental cars, and accommodations. John, Kent, Kim, Jeff, and Robbie were ready to go the distance to Dyersville.

In August 1994, the Nelsons set off from Laramie and Denver to Chicago by air and drove west to Dubuque, where Kent spent a restless night waiting to realize his vision and reach his destination. Lying in his hotel room bed, Kent had a chance to reflect on where his idea had taken him.

"It was pretty uncharacteristic of me," he admitted. "I just chose to go out and take the ride and see where it took me, and that's really not my style. I tend normally to like to know what I'm getting into and where the perimeter is, and on this particular voyage we just sort of flew by the seat of our pants."

The Nelsons set out early and arrived in Dyersville with the morning sun. All Kent's work to make the trip happen paid off with his first view of the Field of Dreams. With Kent beaming, his fellow travelers fell still and silent as they took in what looked like a scene from the film brought to life.

"It was just awesome," Kent recalled. "I can remember that I just felt like I had smiled on the inside of my belly. It was just so serene and so pastoral early in the morning."

"It was really an incredible experience," John said. "The corn was high, and the sight truly was amazing."

"I didn't have any expectations," Kent said simply, searching for words to describe the scene. "I didn't know what I was going to get into; I just wanted to go see what it was about, and it just was so overwhelmingly correct. It was ordered. It was tranquil, and it was happy. It was peaceful, and the corn was the right color, and the grass was the right color. The dirt on the diamond was fine. The plate was just white enough. The back-field screen was shining in the sun, just bright enough. It was just great.

"Your old tummy just flips, and your heart turns, and you just think, 'The magic that we saw on that big screen was re-created again.' The hair on your arm stands up. The saliva dries up in your mouth and you think, 'I am part of a very special evening.' I felt that way coming out of the movie; I felt that way most every day that I put together my letter and then rethought it and reworded it and reworked it and calling people and getting the airplane tickets."

John was similarly impressed. "If a person has read the book or seen the movie, that setting is unique," he said. "There is no other place that you can go and have the same feelings, I don't believe. I was nostalgic. I was in a state of wonderment and appreciation and filled with love for my kids, the family, the grandkids. It's a wonderful opportunity for an old dude."

The Nelsons left their vehicle, gathered up bats, gloves, and balls, and, as John remembered, "just kind of took over a part of the field."

For Kent, standing on the field with his father, brother, and sons was truly living a dream. Only one thing was missing. "I wanted to play catch on that field," he said quietly. "The first ball I threw was to my father."

Three generations of Nelsons threw baseballs around the outfield and watched each other fade into the corn. They played catch, talked, and soaked in the atmosphere.

When he visited the Field of Dreams, Kent Nelson was an athletic forty-four-year old whose thinning hair and bookish glasses made him look more like the chiropractor he had become than the college basketball player he once was. Thoughtful and sincere, he basked in warmth of the Iowa morning he was sharing with his family. At seventy, John Nelson combined John Wayne's stature with Karl Malden's features, giving him an appearance of an aging, but able, veteran. Hardened by service in the Marine Corps in the Pacific Theater during World War II and the Korean conflict just a few years later, sharing the moment with sons and grandsons brought out a softness in the former leatherneck.

For the visit, Kent ordered special hats for the group. The black hats were emblazoned with a large white *N* surrounded with a red braid. Below the braid, each hat read "Dream," and above the left ear each hat was personalized with the wearer's name. United with their headgear and bonded by their journey, the fathers and sons engaged in the simple ritual of a game of catch and the more complex conversation it involves.

A boy, a man, two gloves, and a ball comprise the ritual, but those who have used the game of catch to bond understand that the father–son catch can be dialogue, ceremony, and even covenant. Even when the catch is just simple fun, it is something that both father and son look forward to with great expectation.

For Kent, a catch with his father was always a highlight. "Growing up, Dad might be able to get home a little early, and I'd work on pitching. He'd catch me, and we'd throw balls back and forth and say lots by saying very little. I don't know if it ever really got much better," he said. "That was probably . . . the center of my relationship with my dad for a long time. There weren't too many rules. There wasn't a lot said. I remember that fondly. That was good stuff.

"Dad was always willing to go out and catch and throw and throw me grounders. So somewhere in my makeup was something about heaving a ball back and forth with the man. I felt I wanted to do it in Iowa before we might not be together anymore.

"I tried to . . . introduce my children to just the simple joy of throwing that ball back and forth where you didn't have to say a lot but just because you were with somebody else whom you cared about."

There were a few lumps in throats as the Nelsons played catch, hit fungos, shagged flies, and slid around in the outfield. "I felt a certain closeness that five males could have in a strange part of the world and really it was just heaving that little baseball around that made us all the same," said Kent. "I'm not sure that, as the eldest son, I wasn't doing a little bit of micromanipulation. I think that I felt that the tradition of playing catch with my father was so rich to me that I wanted that for my brother, and if he didn't have it with my dad growing up, maybe I could share that experience with my brother and my father on that same turf. And I felt being fortunate enough to be the father of two young children, maybe I could plant a seed for them, and maybe through their life they could turn to playing catch and have it do for them what it had done for me.

"Watching out for all the others involved in the day, I felt that I played a small role in putting those four people together in a special spot of the world and then just step back and let the simplicity and the beauty of playing catch knit them together and I think that happened. That's as good a feeling as I've had in my life trying to amalgamate something and share it with somebody else and pass that baton."

Before they left Dyersville, Kent watched his father and brother share an embrace. For Kent, watching the show of emotion between two men he had not known to display their feelings was a treat. "I looked up on that old Iowa street and saw Kim go over and hug my dad," Kent said. "I felt like that was a proper place for that to have taken place. I was pleased that that occurred."

Similarly, Kent's sons got a chance to see a side of their father that they did not often see. Gratified, Kent recalled, "My sons, I believe, got a chance to perhaps see a little bit more 'Dad being natural' than they perhaps were accustomed to seeing. I got to be about what I wanted to be out there."

John said simply, "It was just a wonderful, marvelous experience. It was a lot of sentimentality that was involved, a lot of hilarity. My goodness, what greater privilege could a father ever have than to make a trip like that with his two sons and his grandsons? We had a good time at the Field of Dreams."

"I am a better guy for having gone because I think it allowed me to touch some stuff that I hadn't looked at for a long, long time," said Kent. "During the visit, I sensed an electricity, a simplicity."

The Nelsons came to Dyersville as a family but soon realized that by making the trip, they became part of a larger clan. Kent observed the gathering of visitors on the field and understood the connection. "I saw a lot of laughter," he said. "I saw a lot of smiles. I sensed that this was a part of the world that could do something pretty interesting to a lot of people, and though we didn't know anybody else, there was a certain kindred association that we felt."

But the trip was also a very personal experience within the group experience. "I treasure it. It's mine," Kent said. "It is just really an enriching experience to see people all there for whatever reason having a good time, smiling.

"I think it was an opportunity for me and countless other people who have made the journey to . . . look at what was important to us at one point in our life and hold it up in Dyersville, Iowa, and see that lots of other people did something similar and find out it was good. And we were validated for having those beliefs."

John concurred. "I think without a question that it is the expectancy of actually being there that heightens the deal," he said. "There's no question in my mind that it was multiplied many times, the feeling and the excitement, being on the field. All of those feelings are enhanced in that setting."

Those feelings do not have to remain in Iowa. "I made a promise to myself when I was on the field that I would tell a lot more people that I loved them," Kent recalled. "I told myself that I would play catch a whole bunch more, and I told myself that the people that I had deemed to be important in my life were going to be important in my life, and I was going to put a lot more of me into them."

John Nelson returned home from his visit to the Field of Dreams with a thought that others would travel to Dyersville. "I told my wife a little bit ago, 'I think this place very well may become a shrine.'"

While he never thought that his dad was very emotional, Kent has seen him choke up a bit when talking about the trip. "My dad spoke of that experience with a lot of his friends for a good number of months, and I was always buoyed by his willingness to share," Kent said.

But Kent and John are not too quick to tell others of the experience, fearing that they would be seen as bragging to describe their remarkable experience. "It's such an unbelievable experience that it's hard to know who to share it with, so we've shared it very few people other than our very closest friends," said John. "It'd almost be like you're showing off or bragging, and we wouldn't like to do that."

Although concerns for his father's health have often occupied his thoughts since his trip to the Field of Dreams, the reminders of the journey are both tangible and intangible. So Kent now often looks at the glove he used in Iowa and remembers the trip, he treasures the relationships with his family, and he thinks of the baseball diamond in the cornfield. "I will return to Dyersville," he declares. "My father is welcome to join me if he wants to go. But I can draw from Dyersville in Lakewood, Colorado, playing some catch with him outside. And we have."

Of his father, Kent speaks simply with emotion choking his words, "He's a good man. He's been a good friend."

Of the son who made the trip to the Field of Dreams real, John said softly, "He's been a thoughtful, considerate son all of his life. Sometimes he's been so good that I wondered who his father was.

"We all think we've been pretty good fathers until we see someone like him. I didn't know anything about being a good father compared to the job that he's doing with his youngsters."

Measuring his words as they threatened to crack with emotion, John spoke of his son, "He's an outstanding man."

Advising sons contemplating a trip to the Field of Dreams or some similar experience with their fathers, John offered, "This is an opportunity to open up some avenues, communication, feeling, and memories that probably could only be accomplished in that setting. It was a special time."

But as a word of warning to other sons who contemplate making the journey with their fathers—either the actual trip to Dyersville or the gesture of reaching out to their dads—Kent counseled, "Don't wait too long."

Moved by the emotions he felt from watching a film and reading a book, Kent Nelson gathered three generations of his family hundreds of miles from their homes to play catch on a baseball diamond in an Iowa cornfield. More than just an opportunity to have a catch, the trip allowed the Nelsons to express how much they meant to each other. Fathers and sons told each other "I love you" on a baseball field while the sentiment might have seemed elusive elsewhere. Grown men told themselves that they were going to make an effort to show their loved ones how they feel.

FATHERS, SONS, AND BASEBALL

The Field of Dreams has certainly become a favorite destination for movie buffs looking to extend their connection to a favorite film, for individuals looking for something simple in a hectic world, for seekers of the sacred in a secular society, and for people looking for a second chance in an unforgiving world. But for fathers and sons, the *Field of Dreams* movie set has, indeed, achieved shrinelike status. Hollywood's version of W. P. Kinsella's tale may have been fantasy, but Dyersville's Field of Dreams has inspired a very real response in visitors from across the globe. With its connection to the national pastime and the moving film, it has been able to help fathers and sons communicate and bond.

The Field of Dreams is actually tailor-made for fathers and sons with dimensions that allow the younger generation and the over-the-hill set to knock one into the corn. With its shallow home-run distances, the field cries out for everyone young and old to swing for the corn.

For men and boys who often find common ground elusive and communication rare, the combination of the popularity of baseball and the message of *Field of Dreams* makes the movie site a natural attraction to those who need a catalyst or conduit for words and feelings that remain bottled up in other venues.

Baseball has truly marked the passage of time in America—especially for fathers and sons. Baseball captivated the nation and helped to bridge the gap between aging men and their adolescent sons for generations before other major team sports reached the national consciousness.

In the film, Terence Mann states:

I don't have to tell you that the one constant through all the years has been baseball. America has rolled by like an army of steamrollers. It's been erased like a blackboard, rebuilt and erased again. But baseball has marked time. This field, this game . . . it's a piece of our past. It reminds us of all that once was good and it could be again.

Mann turns out to be prophetic. The Field of Dreams has connected with baseball fans and other for whom the game of baseball represents a bond from generation to generation. Perhaps more than any other diversion, baseball has proven its consistent ability to link young and old and form bonds where other communication fails. Time honored and timeless, baseball has proven its ability to invite conversation.

Historian Ken Burns looked at baseball's ability to connect generations and questioned, "What encodes and stores the genetic material of our civilization—passing down to the next generation the best of us, what we hope will mutate into betterness for our children and our posterity?" He responded definitively, "Baseball provides one answer. Nothing in our daily life offers more of the comfort of continuity, the generational connection of belonging to a vast and complicated American family, the powerful sense of home, the freedom from time's constraints, and the great gift of accumulated memory than does our National Pastime."

For W. P. Kinsella, "Baseball is a thinking person's game. It's the ballet of sports, the chess of sports. There are all the permutations and combinations of what can possibly happen next. The thing that attracts writers to baseball is the openendedness of the game. The other sports are all twice enclosed—first by time and then by rigid playing boundaries."

In *Shoeless Joe,* Kinsella writes, "Growing up is a ritual—more deadly than religion, more complicated than baseball, for there seem to be no rules. Everything is experienced for the first time. But baseball can soothe even those pains, for it is stable and permanent, steady as a grandfather dozing on a wicker chair on a verandah." He accurately captures the difficulty of aging. Just when people have one stage of life figured out—how to be a kid, how to be a parent of a young child—they must enter the next stage and learn anew, how to be a young adult, how to be a parent of an adolescent. Anything, even baseball, can be a comfort if it can provide some stability as they grow.

BASEBALL'S CULTURAL OMNIPRESENCE

In *The National Game: Baseball and American Culture*, author John Rossi declares, "Baseball has formed an intimate link with American history and culture for more than a century and a half. No other sport has imbedded itself so deeply in the national psyche or has generated such a large body of serious literature."

American high and popular culture is overflowing with baseball. Baseball writing can be a fawning biography or a superficial recount of a season of glory, but at its best, it takes its place in the literary pantheon. In prose, baseball literature is John Updike, writing of Ted Williams's reluctance to take a curtain call after hitting a home run in his final at bat: "Gods do not answer letters." In fiction, it is Bernard Malamud, writing of the fictional hero Roy Hobbs who, when confronted by a fan who does not believe his hero let him down, "lifted his hands to his face and wept many bitter tears." As if the sport's association with American literature needs additional certification, note that the very tome entitled *The Great American Novel* is a book about baseball. With homage to *Moby Dick*, Philip Roth's story begins "Call Me Smitty" and regales readers with humorous tales of the fictional Patriot League.

In film, from *Bang the Drum Slowly* to *The Bad News Bears*, baseball has been a consistent source of inspiration for Hollywood and a regular source of entertainment for moviegoers. The scenes of Gary Cooper delivering the doomed Lou Gehrig's "luckiest man on the face of the Earth" speech in *The Pride of the Yankees* and Robert Redford circling the bases before a shower of pyrotechnics in *The Natural* are classic images from the silver screen.

In poetry, there is Ernest Lawrence Thayer's *Casey at the Bat;* on Broadway, *Damn Yankees;* in song, from *Take Me Out to the Ballgame* to *Centerfield*, baseball provides a soundtrack that can last for an entire season. Other sports have their occasional appearance in nonsport media, but only baseball is ubiquitous in every medium.

The national pastime has long since transcended existence as a popular team sport and has become an integral part of the American experience. As the unifying thread connecting the elements of the tale of redemption running through *Field of Dreams*, baseball instantly resonates with those who understand the game and the bond it forms between generations.

John Rossi stated, "Baseball has survived and often prospered largely because for almost two centuries it has been deeply imbedded in America's roots. . . . Knowledge and understanding of the game has been passed from one generation to the next. . . . A person watching a game today is sharing an experience that is little different from what it was more than a century ago. That is not the case with other modern sports in America which bear little resemblance to their beginnings."

In costume and conduct, baseball today resembles baseball of decades ago much more than any other major team sport. By the time basketball was invented by Dr. James Naismith in a Springfield, Massachusetts, YMCA, baseball had already become a staple on the nation's sports pages. Baseball team names like the Cincinnati Reds, Philadelphia Phillies, and Chicago Cubs had long been established before the National Football League was created. The first World Series championship had been claimed years before the National Hockey League took to the ice.

Similarly, more than any other sporting arena, the baseball field is an identifiable portrait. From the uniquely shaped home plate, to the recognizable layout of the infield, to the sharp straightness of the foul lines in contrast with the bow of the outfield, the baseball field is a prototypical form. Fly over any populated area in the United States, and every baseball field is instantly identifiable. Other sporting fields, shopping centers, and houses dot the landscape, but the ballfield will stand out from all but the highest altitude. At the Field of Dreams, the attractiveness of the message and the association of the "dreams can come true" message with the icon that is the baseball field create a powerful draw. It taps into people's deepest longings and America's national consciousness at the same time.

Generations of parents and their children had grown old and passed on a love of baseball before the other major sports of the modern era began to eat into its prevalence. Despite the growing popularity of other sports, the competition from a myriad of alternate forms of entertainment, and baseball's own foibles that sometimes seem intent on destroying the game itself, the baseball game is firmly established in the national consciousness and securely rooted in American culture.

Still, some wonder whether baseball's importance to the national psyche or its ability to connect the generations could be on the wane. While it retains a strong fan base, the demand for baseball—and sports in general—might be perilously close to dropping below its supply. Baseball's television ratings have declined, but with so many channels competing for viewers, that is not necessarily an indication of a decline in interest. Major League Baseball attendance has increased in recent years, especially as the majors have expanded. But with fans in small markets fully aware that only the most free-spending teams have a chance to win the World Series, the sport could face a crisis in maintaining fan interest. As the surging economy that has helped to fuel the expansion of team revenues and players' salaries slows, American sports in general, and baseball specifically, could face a crisis.

Baseball's fan base is heavy with aging men who grew up idolizing Willie Mays and Mickey Mantle and thinking of the game as somehow removed from the business realities that have threatened it in recent years. Young fans seek sporting entertainment that fits their need for instant gratification, and many of their parents are disillusioned by baseball's recent labor–management strife.

As fewer children grow up with two parents in the same house and more kids are more likely to play video baseball than to take the field, it is unclear that baseball will be a unifier of families into the future. With the hectic pace of modern society, some even suggest that playing catch is thought of as a duty more than a pleasure for new parents.

In his book *Imagining Baseball*, David McGimpsey writes, "That baseball has become a celebrated metaphor for America is already old news.

Like soda pop and the open road, baseball has inspired a distinctive series of patriotic and nostalgic fictions, which have long been popular. Celebrated by fans as one of the best and most American of American things, baseball is thought to be a peculiarly affirming pursuit."

But McGimpsey questions baseball's place in the popular culture, suggesting, "As fewer people care who won last night, baseball continues to aspire to its own fiction." Following that logic, it is clear that the myth making and sugarcoating of baseball is encouraged by the lords of the game to help set the game apart from other diversions. Baseball's ties to the popular culture and its strong base of romanticized fiction help sell the game as they reinforce the soft version of the game in films, literature, and poetry.

In a July 1989 essay in *The New Yorker*, Roger Angell commented, "I like baseball, the game and the games, but I can't always understand why it's so hard to look at the pastime with a clear gaze. We seem to want to go on sweetening it up, frosting the flakes, because we want it to say things about ourselves that probably aren't true."

THE GAME AS A VEHICLE
Had the same tale of redemption played out in a film about football or basket weaving, it simply could not have resonated as strongly with as large of an audience. By using baseball, *Shoeless Joe* and *Field of Dreams* find an instantly receptive audience just as certainly as Mary Poppins's spoonful of sugar helps the medicine go down.

The director of *Field of Dreams* understands baseball's allure. "There's something about baseball that touches feelings about growing up," Robinson said. "I was not a great player, but I learned so much through the game. Most of all, I learned about life—how you win some, you lose some. Baseball has a long season; you're in it for the long haul. It's like the voice that calls to the protagonist: 'Go the distance.' It's the stuff of which myths are made."

The director has noted the ability of his imagery to create a powerful response. Speaking of the reaction, Robinson said, "I know I have gotten a ton of mail from people all over the world talking about how the film has reconciled families—very emotional letters and many of them surprisingly similar that begin with, 'I haven't spoken to my father in twenty years and when I saw your movie, I called him up and said, "Dad, let's have a catch," or "Come see this movie with me."' I suspect the phenomenon of the field is an adjunct of that."

Robinson also understands the simple attraction of having a catch. "My favorite childhood memories—and they're not extraordinary moments—they're either sitting around the dinner table or being out in the backyard having a catch with my dad. There's something very lovely about a warm summer night, a little boy throwing a ball back and forth with his dad—a lovely American ritual, part of growing up. I think that the movie certainly was informed by knowledge of how lovely a memory that is. I guess the field is sort of a [symbol] for many people of that. Even for a cynic like me who does not believe that you can go into the past and touch things, it's a lovely fantasy. We'd like to believe we could."

Field of Dreams' tearjerker ending was actually tweaked to make it clear to all that Ray Kinsella was having a catch with his father. In the original screenplay, Ray Kinsella initiated the catch by asking simply, "You wanna have a catch?" But after test audiences didn't respond to the scene to Robinson's liking, the director added the two words "Hey, Dad" to the line to make it clear that the audience was witnessing the father–son reunion.

The ritual of the father–son catch actually comprises much more than a simple warm-up. The building of a bond, the measuring of growing skills, and the ability to engage in meaningful interaction without need for words are all wrapped up in the simple back-and-forth. For any father who bought his infant son a glove, only to endure the wait until his son was old enough to use it, and for any son who has longed to reestablish the connection built through years of playing catch, the film *Field of Dreams* and the Dyersville movie site evoke powerful memories.

In his essay "Fathers Playing Catch with Sons," poet Donald Hall recounts, "My father and I played catch as I grew up. Like so much else between fathers and sons, playing catch was tender and terse at the same time. He wanted to play with me. He wanted me to be good. He seemed to *demand* that I be good."

Hall declares, "Baseball connects American males with each other, not only through bleacher friendships and neighbor loyalties, not only through barroom fights but, most importantly, through generations. When you are small, you may not discuss politics or union dues or profit margins with your father's cigar-smoking friends when your father has gone out for a six-pack, but you may discuss baseball."

Bob Boone has the distinction of being part of a three-generation Major League Baseball family, the son of infielder Ray Boone and father of infielders Bret and Aaron Boone. In his nineteen-year Major League Baseball career, the able backstop was selected to four All-Star teams, won seven gold gloves, earned a World Series ring with the 1980 Philadelphia Phillies, and went on to manage the Kansas City Royals and Cincinnati Reds. Boone grew up as the son of a major league father and raised two major league sons. What is it about baseball that connects fathers and sons? Boone answered simply, "You can have a catch with your son."

"Baseball has been a tremendous vehicle for my wife and me," Boone shared. Allowing some fatherly pride, he beamed of his sons, "Baseball is a vehicle that brought them through adolescence. They're good citizens, and they weren't trapped in a lot of the things that are out there to trap you, and baseball is a big reason for that."

What is it about baseball that joins the generations? "Events usually trigger memories of feelings that we like to relive and other feelings we don't like to relive," Boone suggests. "Baseball is a catalyst for that."

Of fathers and sons, the man who can speak as a major league father and a major league son suggests that the baseball diamond and the ballpark are sanctuaries for fathers and sons. "That's where dad and son can go hang out, talk, sit there and argue, and actually have a conversation," he said. "That's one of the hard things to do—father and son—is have a conversation about things in life because they have to be initiated. Baseball somehow forces it, and baseball is a microcosm of life."

James Earl Jones sees the link between America's pastime and its fathers and sons. "It's about the communion between father and son, the father being the secondary parent up to a point," he stated. "About the time that a kid can catch a baseball, that phenomenon in the back yard happens . . . and it's sort of the first communion: 'Let's play catch.' There is a great strong bond between two people playing catch. It might be casual. It could be intense. But there's always a bond, and I think that's the first bond that a male child has with a male parent."

For one who has not had that bond, the long-term ramifications can be significant. *Dreamfield* executive producer Tim Crescenti confessed that he and his father "never had that catch." In fact, when Tim wanted to play little league, his father refused. It was not that Tim's father had anything against baseball, but he had involved Tim's older brother with little league and was appalled by parents' squabbling and the disappointing conduct of those who attended the games. So Tim was not involved in little league. But what may have been a one-time disappointment lingered into adulthood.

After his second trip to the Field of Dreams, while he was still pondering what he would do with his inspiration for a documentary, he was struck with a thought. "I realized, 'Y'know what, I need to go see my dad and I need to resolve my catch with him,'" he said. "I had a wonderful father, but it was always one little thorn in the side of me of why he would never let me play baseball and why I never had that catch."

He drove eight hours to his father's home in Arizona and spoke to his dad in his woodworking shop where he was making a stool for Crescenti's own son. Tim's father explained that the decision not to let Tim play baseball was not about denying him a pleasurable experience but about not exposing him to an unpleasant environment.

Crescenti asked his father to have that catch. Focused on his wood-work, his father balked, still not understanding the meaning of the request. But even though he was rebuffed, Tim developed a new under-standing of his father. Watching his father carefully handcrafting a gift to his grandson, Tim saw that the act of woodworking was his father's way of having a catch—of making the bond and of expressing his love through an action.

A year after the debut of *Dreamfield*, Crescenti was able to visit the Field of Dreams with his wife, children, and father while working on another project. Standing on the Field of Dreams at age thirty-four, he finally had his first catch with his father. "That was just one of the greatest times of my life," he said. "To be at that field and to throw a ball with my dad and just talk to him, and then he turned and threw to my son and then threw to my daughter. That was just the best."

When his father died a few years later, Crescenti was, of course, saddened but also thankful that he finally had been able to resolve his issues and find a way to appreciate his father and how he showed his emotions.

Field of Dreams visitor Vinnie Caruso had a similar tale—one that still wants for a happy ending. "My dad never played catch with me," he said. "I don't know what it was—either he was with the guys or he felt indifferent. Whatever the reason, he would never play catch with me."

When he saw *Field of Dreams*, he said, "The ending just hit me like a ton of bricks. Every time we looked at it—just hit me like a ton of bricks because I wish my dad could play catch with me."

Although Caruso's father was still relatively young and able—not yet a senior citizen when *Field of Dreams* debuted—he continued to refuse his son's request. He never watched the film. He never even unwrapped the copy of the film his son gave him.

"He doesn't understand how much of a bonding we could actually have if we could play catch and by watching the movie," Vinnie said, ruefully. While he waits to have his catch with his father, he plays catch with his understanding wife and eager dogs. "I still yearn—maybe one day I can play catch with my dad—but one of these days I'm going to have to face the truth and say, 'You know it's not going to happen.'"

Like the musical give-and-take of "Dueling Banjos," the baseball catch is like a conversation. One throw yields a response. A soft toss is like an invitation; a harder throw, like a challenge. Without words, the interaction is both expressive and meaningful.

Baseball is not an easy game to learn, and it is not an easy game to appreciate. Baseball skills must be taught. From the unnatural motion of throwing overhand, to the hazardous act of fielding a ground ball, to the frustrating experience of attempting to hit the spherical baseball with the cylindrical bat, baseball is all about developing muscle memory and hand–eye coordination and enduring trial and error until success is achieved. Learning the nuances of the rules, the logic of the strategies, and the lore of the game make developing a mind for baseball a lifelong activity.

Enthusiasts of other sports will consider it a gross simplification, but the fact is that one can throw a soccer ball onto a lawn, and young children will be able to almost instinctively imitate the rudimentary kicking and trapping skills of soccer; one can show a child a basketball and a hoop and the child can begin heaving ball at basket with enthusiasm. But for baseball, a child needs instruction and a partner who can instruct how to throw, catch, and hit and who can be a partner who can play catch, hit balls, and pitch. Young children can have fun seconds after being introduced to some sports. Baseball does not become fun until a young player has developed a rudimentary competence in some of the skills required to play the game.

Thus, baseball skills and an appreciation for the game must be taught and learned. It is a game that demands a connection from one to another—perhaps parent to child—to initiate facility and develop competency. Then, to appreciate the subtleties of baseball, the game reinforces that connection as understanding and awareness grow.

A GIRL'S BEST FRIEND?

In *Wait till Next Year: A Memoir*, historian and oft-heartbroken Brooklyn Dodgers and Boston Red Sox fan Doris Kearns Goodwin writes, "I feel an invisible bond between our three generations, an anchor of loyalty linking my sons to the grandfather whose face they never saw but whose person they have already come to know through this most timeless of all sports, the game of baseball." While Goodwin understands the connection between American males and baseball, many women find the link elusive.

After the May 1989 debut of *Field of Dreams*, the women's magazine *Mademoiselle* tried to answer the question "What *is* it with guys and baseball?" Writer Ron Rosenbaum recounted a woman friend's bitter denouncement of the film as ridiculous and nonsensical and her angry questioning of why men fight back tears during screenings. He then set out to answer the question that has frustrated so many females. "*Field of Dreams* gets to the heart of the lifelong bond American men feel for the game," Rosenbaum stated. Claiming that many American males retain the romantic, quixotic streak displayed by Kevin Costner's Ray Kinsella, Rosenbaum described the chance to take on "one last shot" at a quest as incredibly attractive. The feeling of "wanting one last shot at getting it right with your dad," Rosenbaum said, is "something practically every guy in America suffers from."

In the end, the explanation touched on the catch. "Playing catch with your father is sort of the primal way American fathers and sons relate," Rosenbaum wrote. "It's perfect—nonverbal communication. . . . Tossing a ball back and forth with your father, relating in the disguise of learning baseball from him, is probably the most universal experience of father–son communion American men and boys have. . . . It's silent bonding in the form of baseball. It's repressed but, hey, we like it that way."

According to a multimarket study conducted by Major League Baseball in 2000, women declared that baseball was their favorite among all professional sports to watch on television and to attend in person.

The same survey indicated that women make up 46 percent of the attendance at Major League Baseball games. This cross-gender appeal, however, does not necessarily translate into an understanding of the bond the game forms between fathers and sons.

Pitcher Ila Borders became the first woman to pitch and win a men's professional baseball game when she played in the independent Northern League, debuting in 1997 and earning her first win in 1998. With her unique perspective, Borders can add some insight. Speaking specifically of the male connection with baseball films and the game itself, Borders suggested, "I think it's because they try to live their life through what they're watching—those players out on the field or that movie—they tap in. They think that's part of them, it's obtainable, whereas women, I don't think, see that as being obtainable."

What about the Field of Dreams? Is it just a field? It is not just a field to baseball players, not to Borders. "I don't see it like that," she said. "Every baseball field I go onto, as soon as I step my foot on the playing field, I don't care where it's at, something magical happens. To have a baseball field out of nowhere, something like that is just heavenly."

OF RICE AND CORN

If the connection between men and baseball is not intuitive to most women, the connection is certainly not necessarily limited to American males. In fact, the Field of Dreams phenomenon itself is not just an American tale. Visitors from across the globe have traveled to Dyersville as tourists, and the film and its message have found a special following in Japan.

As one of the most successful foreign films in Japanese history, *Field of Dreams* played to packed movie houses and enthusiastic crowds. Unlike American audiences, however, the Japanese knew what to expect. The text on Japanese movie posters teased the notion that "lost people come back" and noted that "led by a mysterious voice, [Ray Kinsella] meets his 21-year-old father in the blowing wind of an Iowa cornfield." So not only was the ending not a total surprise, it was used to attract moviegoers.

Given Japanese culture's embrace of baseball and its reverence toward deceased ancestors, *Field of Dreams* was a natural hit in the Land
of the Rising Sun. It only made sense that visitors from Japan, where
pilgrimages to shrines are common, soon began journeying to Dyersville. Since the film's 1990 premiere in Tokyo, Japanese visitors to the
field have been common, and mentions of the field in Japanese media
have been frequent.

Just as Americans have a love of the pastoral, there is a soft spot in
the collective Japanese heart for the countryside. In an era when rural
farming communities are fading away as young residents leave for jobs
in cities, the Japanese see the disappearance of its farming culture as a
loss of an entire way of life. In a culture that loves baseball, cherishes
a disappearing agrarian life, and is fascinated with things American,
Dyersville's Field of Dreams and the film that inspired it have become
icons.

A Japanese freelance copywriter took that love and fascination and
created a homage to *Field of Dreams* and the Field of Dreams movie
set. Inspired by the film and passionate about baseball, Haruyoshi Hori
turned a rice paddy in Takamiya, a small village north of Hiroshima,
into a baseball field surrounded by a crop of corn.

Not only was Hori enthralled by the film's interpretation of the
spirituality of baseball and its combination of Americana and sentimentality, he was impressed with the story of how the Iowa farmers
maintained the Field of Dreams in Dyersville. A lifelong baseball
player and fan who grew up in Tokyo, Hori organized a band of
fellow enthusiasts who raised funds and toiled together to realize the
inspired vision.

In *Field of Dreams*, Ray Kinsella seems almost effortlessly to build
his field single-handedly in a montage of short scenes that take up only
moments on the screen. The Hollywood-led effort to construct the set
for the film on the Lansing and Ameskamp land was completed over
a long weekend by dozens of laborers. Hori's group, however, labored
on weekends and during spare time for about one full year, smoothing

and draining a terraced rice paddy, creating the field, and tending a rare cornfield in Japan.

Hori's group intentionally avoided using heavy machinery, preferring to create their vision by hand. When completed, Hori's field was a hardscrabble but perfectly functional baseball diamond with grass more sparse than lush and grounds that are more untamed than manicured. Unlike its Dyersville counterpart, which is surrounded by crops and rather isolated from signs of modern life, a busy highway runs just beyond Hori's right field, and a number of buildings encroach upon the diamond. While it may not have been postcard-picturesque when completed, the field had an obviously handcrafted charm. Like any good work of art, Hori's creation was "signed" with a prominent marker that declares "Dream Field 1995.9.3" in bright yellow English letters against a green background.

On the field's opening day, Hori's baseball team, the Corns, emerged triumphantly from their cornfield and made a giddy dash toward the diamond. After fielding a ground ball at third base and making the play for an out, Hori reportedly shouted, "There's nothing more I need to do. Now I can die."

Hori's field has attracted a small stream of tourists, but exists mainly for the enjoyment of the Corns. In 1996, as part of a tour of Japan, Dyersville's Ghost Players met the Corns on Hori's field. Although the Americans won the contest, the Japanese players were thrilled to be honored with a visit from the team from Dyersville, some of whom were recognizable, not from their small roles in *Field of Dreams* but from an appearance the Ghost Players made in a Japanese rock video. After enjoying the Corns' Japanese hospitality and the game on Hori's field, the Ghost Players complimented their hosts and their efforts to create their ballfield. Hori was delighted to hear the Ghost Players declare that he had done a "good job."

Ghost Player Keith Rahe described the difference between Dyersville's Field of Dreams and Hori's Dream Field. "This is a nice place," Rahe said of the Dyersville movie site. "But Hollywood spent hundreds of thousands of dollars to make it that way. These people did it all with their own hands. In one sense it probably was more of a true field of dreams because it was those people's dream to build that diamond and play ball there."

Rahe's Ghost Players entertain visitors with their genuinely funny, Harlem Globetrotter–like performance at the Field of Dreams on the last Sunday of each month from June through September. But the show hasn't stopped at the foul lines. These Dyersville area farmers, professionals, and weekend ballplayers in classic baseball uniforms have parlayed their steady Field of Dreams gig into worldwide notoriety. The Ghost Players have been invited to travel to across the globe to perform for *Field of Dreams* fans and baseball enthusiasts. In addition to their trip to Japan, the Ghost Players have criss-crossed the country and entertained American troops in Cuba and Europe. The Ghost Players have been featured in numerous national print publications and television commercials. Created to entertain at the Field of Dreams, the Ghost Players have been able to extend the fame of the film through their act and bring a bit of the magic from the corn to the world.

Without the film *Field of Dreams* and its vestigial movie locale, the men who portray the Ghost Players would be farmers, professionals, and ordinary weekend ballplayers. Through the interest created by the *Field of Dreams* movie site, these men have found a vicarious fame that has turned them into world-traveling, autograph-signing all-stars.

As part of their tour of Japan, the Ghost Players encountered Seigo Yamada who, as a player, helped a team from Nagasaki defeat the visitors from Dyersville and, as an English speaker, helped the Ghost Players with their cross-cultural communication. Yamada has even visited Dyersville to emerge from the corn in a 1919 White Sox uniform as a Ghost Player. Remarking on the popularity of the field for Japanese visitors, he said, "They miss the good old days when father was father and mother was mother . . . because the Japanese society is becoming such a busy society and the sons and daughters are losing quality time with their parents."

Yamada noted that the love of baseball and the sport's ability to connect generations are not the only ideas that cross over from American to Japanese culture. Jealousy apparently resonates just as well. Describing his friends' reaction to his experiences emerging from the Dyersville corn to interact with visitors on the Field of Dreams, Yamada laughed, "They are green with envy."

Takeshi Horie and Kuniyuki Shibuya visited the Field of Dreams in 2000. From Osaka, Japan, they traveled halfway across the globe—more than seventeen hours in transit each way—to fulfill their dream. Noting that he saw the film *Field of Dreams* in junior high school, Takeshi gushed that he had waited more than a decade to make his trip. He did not visit the United States to see the Statue of Liberty or the Grand Canyon. As a baseball fan, Takeshi happily passed over significant attractions and natural wonders to see the Field of Dreams. He admitted that some friends may have thought he was a little crazy to travel from Japan to Iowa for a few days at the famous field, but he defended his trip by stating simply, "Our dream is to come here."

In *Shoeless Joe*, Ray Kinsella ponders what he thinks will happen as he, his twin brother, and their father take the first steps toward repairing their father–son bonds. "As the three of us walk across the vast emerald lake that is the outfield, I think of all the things I'll want to talk to the catcher about," Kinsella ponders. "I'll guide the conversations, like taking a car around a long, gentle curve in the road, and we'll hardly realize that we're talking of love, and family, and life, and beauty, and friendship, and sharing."

The fictional Kinsella understands that baseball is much more than just a pastime for those who love the game. He knew that talk of baseball is more than sports and that discussions surrounding baseball—like the baseball catch—are much more complex than a simple back-and-forth toss.

For many sons who have been unable to tell their fathers how they feel away from the field, a trip to Dyersville has served as a love letter. The visit helps communicate, "Dad, I wish I could say all that I feel, but

I can't—but know that I feel for you, all of the strong emotions I feel when I watch *Field of Dreams*."

But baseball, the film, and the field can only initiate the conversation. It is up to the fathers and sons—or families or friends—themselves to capitalize on the connection. By using the universality of baseball to connect the generations, fathers and sons have found that the film *Field of Dreams* is a spark and the movie site a catalyst that can initiate conversations that, perhaps, cannot begin elsewhere.

So maybe dreams really do come true. Maybe art imitates life. Maybe there is magic in the corn. And maybe a former movie set in Dyersville, Iowa, is heaven.

Is This Heaven?

"Is this heaven?"

—*"Shoeless" Joe Jackson*

"No. It's Iowa."

—*Ray Kinsella*

When Jim Bohn visited the Field of Dreams, he sought to reconnect with his dead son and find some closure a year after the plane crash that changed his family forever. More than a decade after his trip to Dyersville, he reflected on his struggle to come to terms with his son's death, knowing that it is an ordeal he must continue to live with. A visit to the Field of Dreams can bring comfort but cannot totally ease the pain. "Time helps," he said, describing the healing process. "The pain is still there. It's just not as sharp."

Now, Bohn forever connects the movie site and the film *Field of Dreams* with his relationship with his son and his ongoing effort to come to terms with his loss.

"Having been at the field, it makes part of the movie more comforting," he said, his voice cracking with emotion. "The part where Ray has a catch with his dad, when I first saw the movie, I pictured me having a catch with my dad, not Matt having a catch with me—'cause he's one of the ones that plays on that field every day now.

"And then the part at the end where they just show the train of lights, the cars coming in—I was one of them."

Sometimes that emotional reaction to the film and the field can interfere with a healthy perspective on life. This was a realization that Bohn had to come to over time.

"I can remember when I went there, you don't know why all these other people are there, and I'm sure there's people who just come because that's where they made the movie—no other reason," he explained. "When I was there, I'm there with all this deep emotional stuff. People are sitting in the bleachers, and they're just having a jolly good time and they're doing the wave. I didn't remember right quick that they did that in the movie—that Ray and Annie are sitting up there and they do the wave. And I looked over and I thought, 'What are these people doing? What's wrong with you? Don't you know what kind of a place this is?' And then I caught myself and I said, 'No, Jim, this is not a church. This is not some solemn, holy place. This is like an anything kind of place. Whatever you want it to be.' And after I said that to myself, I kind of smiled and said, 'Yeah, this is not "Come here and be sad and cry"; this is "Come here and be happy and open yourself up to whatever is going to happen."'"

Similarly, Bohn reflected on his interpretation of the film. "This movie means different things to you, it means different things to other people," he said. Some people just don't see the deeper meaning in this movie. They just take it on the surface, and they don't get the connection. Don't argue with them; just let them be the way they are. I can remember feeling that this is my movie—'You're making fun of my movie.'"

The trip to the Field of Dreams was an important part of the healing process for Jim Bohn, but he had no delusions about the power of the location, which—he recognizes—clearly comes from within. "I'm not going to say that there's magic powers or anything about it," he said thoughtfully. "But it has qualities because of the premise around the movie; the whole story about the movie that 'If you build it, he will come.'

"If you believe, then it'll happen. Because you'll make it happen. Because you believe it, you will do things that will make it happen. You may not be conscious of what you are doing, but you will behave, or do, or say—it will make it happen. I'm not going to say what's going to happen, but I'd say something's going to happen."

At the end of *Field of Dreams*, reunited father and son Ray and John Kinsella consider whether the magical field is truly paradise.

"Is this heaven?" John asks plaintively.

"It's Iowa," Ray responds in the same manner-of-fact way he responded to "Shoeless" Joe Jackson earlier in the film.

"Iowa?"

"Yeah."

"I coulda sworn it was heaven."

Ray considers the exchange and turns to his otherworldly visitor with a question (the screenplay instructs that he ask this question as if he were asking the secret of life). "Is there a heaven?"

"Oh, yeah," John answers. "It's the place dreams come true."

Ray surveys his field, looks toward his house where he sees his wife and daughter playing together on the porch swing, and then concludes, "Maybe this is heaven."

In the conception of W. P. Kinsella, the story of Ray Kinsella and his magical field is a story of a perfect world where one can have a perfect family, resurrect the dead, or play baseball at midnight on the grass of a favorite ballpark. Heaven, thus conceived, does not exist as a cloud-filled realm where winged angels pluck harps but as a state of mind that can be achieved as heaven-on-Earth when life is ideal.

It is a field of grass and dirt like so many others. The Dyersville diamond's plate is sixty feet, six inches away from the pitcher's rubber. The bases are ninety feet apart. But that soil and that Iowa corn is sacred ground for people who visit the site for more than pictures and souvenirs.

Not all things to all people, the Field of Dreams has held a number of different meanings for its visitors who bring their own personal interpretations of the novel *Shoeless Joe*, the film *Field of Dreams*, and life itself. But the image of a magical baseball field where the incredible can come true and where second chances can correct mistakes of a lifetime has proven to be enduring.

So is the baseball diamond in a cornfield paradise? Or, in the parlance of the film and its fans, "Is this heaven?" The simple answer is that the Field of Dreams is not heaven. The more complete answer is that for some, the attraction is just a silly tourist attraction. For others, it is an irresistible curiosity. But, for a significant number of visitors, the ballfield on the Lansing and Ameskamp land is something special—a place where dreams really can come true, a place where blocked emotions can be released, and a place where second chances are second nature.

Of course, skeptics may never acknowledge that the Field of Dreams is anything more than a slightly undersized baseball field needlessly occupying a few acres of Iowa's fertile farmland. But much like any situation that calls for faith, for those who believe, no explanation is necessary; for those who do not believe, no explanation is sufficient.

THE POWER OF AN ICON

Visitors have come to the Field of Dreams for a variety of reasons and have walked away with an astounding array of experiences. Mark Babiarz and his teenage son Christopher Albrecht met for the first time at the magical field where they initiated a process to form father–son bonds in a once-nonexistent relationship. The Nelson family visited the former movie set to strengthen familial ties and employed a simple game of catch to connect three generations. Jerry and Lynn Ryan married and began a life together at the unlikely tourist attraction and returned to recharge their union when they needed to be reminded of what is truly important in life.

It is more than ten years since the debut of *Field of Dreams* and two decades since the publication of *Shoeless Joe*. Yet the phenomenon inspired by the novel, visualized in motion pictures, and then brought to life by the hundreds of thousands of visitors continues.

The filming of *Field of Dreams* brought millions of dollars into the Iowa economy. Beyond the fiscal impact, the film helped change the image of Iowa itself, providing the state with the "Is this heaven? No, it's Iowa" slogan and creating a new, magical attraction for the Hawkeye State.

The ongoing flow of tourists has prolonged the impact of the film. Enjoying the fruits of the tourist trade and general economic expansion, Dyersville has added hotel rooms and eateries. Newly constructed houses along 2nd Avenue, neatly trimmed lawns, and a restored basilica are evidence of Dyersville's recent prosperity. But the visitors themselves are evidence of the magic of the site.

Inspired by the film, many think, "I want to achieve my reconciliation before my loved one passes" or "I want to believe in the magic I saw in the movie." Much like the fictional characters in the 1977 film *Close Encounters of the Third Kind*, the inspired are drawn to a common place where they believe they will be able to resolve issues or relate in a way to fellow visitors. Some then speak of the field and the experience surrounding the visit reverently and note its "religious undertones" or talk of their "need to go back to field" and their quest to "understand its message."

Before getting married at the Field of Dreams, Jerry and Lynn Ryan took their film-inspired quest to Wyoming to visit the Devil's Tower National Monument—the site that was the destination for the characters of *Close Encounters of the Third Kind*.

In an original poem, Jerry Ryan described the Field of Dreams as follows:

A moonlit chapel
Three days east
of Devil's Tower

He concludes his ode by describing the Dyersville attraction as

Neither heaven
nor Iowa

As life is
neither movie
Nor parentheses
But rather what shines
Between the baselines
And once around the horn
Rollicking between rows
And spiritual shadows
Of the plainly delighted,
Yet raucously uninvited,
Ty Cobb on the corn.

While filming *Field of Dreams*, Burt Lancaster said, "In dreams, there is the reality that you are looking for. It becomes a reality when you embrace that dream and attempt to realize it."

One of Dyersville's visitors' guides notes of the field, "The farm has drawn visitors not only because of the movie's popularity, but because they feel the magic themselves." They come to find a catalyst that can help them create the change they desire. They come to find a metaphor that will help them speak when they cannot find the vocabulary. They come to find a conduit through which their feelings can flow when they are blocked at home. They come to find a vehicle that can carry emotions too heavy to be expressed in words alone. Some even venture to the Field of Dreams for "guidance" and pause in quiet reflection as they search in the corn and within themselves for answers.

The Field of Dreams cannot slow the pace of this hectic world, but it has helped visitors focus on what is important in life. It cannot push people toward religion, but it has pointed visitors toward the spiritual in a world that increasingly turns toward the secular for guidance. It cannot mend rent relationships, but it has helped visitors take the first steps toward reconciliation. It cannot connect fathers to sons, but it has provided visitors with the foundation that can allow that bond to flourish.

It is somehow fitting that the pilgrimage to Dyersville has been inspired by a creation of Hollywood, since the entertainment industry drives American—and international—popular culture. In 1957, Mircea Eliade wrote in *The Sacred and the Profane*, "A whole volume could well be written on the myths of modern man, on the mythologies camouflaged in the plays that he enjoys, in the books that he reads. The cinema, that 'dream factory,' takes over and employs countless mythical motifs—the fight between hero and monster, initiatory combats and ordeals, paradigmatic figures and images (the maiden, the hero, the paradisal landscape, hell, and so on)."

Moviemakers clearly know what people want. They want the fantasies Hollywood creates. They want to believe in that magic, they want to believe in those second chances, and so they cross their fingers, wear lucky shirts, and travel to the Field of Dreams. From the reporters who have used it for feature articles, to the former major league players who have traveled to Iowa to play in benefit games, to the visitors who journeyed for miles just to slide in its dirt, the field has left its impression on those who have stepped between its chalk lines. Many own videotapes of *Field of Dreams*, collect memorabilia connected to the film, display souvenirs from Dyersville, or even incorporate the film into their identities. A scan of e-mail addresses adopted by Field of Dreams visitors includes the monikers dreams@ . . . , gotoFOD@. . . , or shoeless@. . . .

If imitation is the sincerest form of flattery, then the idea that the Field of Dreams could be duplicated is high praise, indeed. In the film, the magic extended only to boundaries of the baseball diamond. If the magic is confined to the field itself, then it rests in the Iowa soil and waits for visitors to step over the foul lines and feel its power. But if the magic is inspired by the themes of the film and then internalized by viewers, it is possible to replicate the elements of the field in another setting.

Just as Hori Haruyoshi created his field in Japan, baseball fans across the globe have created their own visions of the Field of Dreams in farms and back yards. Just outside Seattle, Washington, the corporate headquarters of a small company that publishes journals for collectors is home to a baseball diamond dubbed "Heaven's Field" that was lovingly laid out over the course of a year and affectionately referred to as "our own 'field of dreams.'" On the Souda Bay Naval Base, the Seabees built the only softball field on the island of Crete and decorated their field with a sign reading, "If you build it, they will come."

Since the debut of the film *Field of Dreams*, it is nearly impossible to read any account of the building of a new baseball field or, for that matter, the building of any attraction—without some reference to the "If you build it . . ." line from the film. In fact, the phrase "If you build it, they will come" has become sufficiently overused that it appears on a list of trite words and phrases to avoid as part of a major American newspaper's official style book. (Interestingly, just as the phrase "Play it again, Sam" was never uttered in *Casablanca*, most people misstate the *Field of Dreams* phrase as "If you build it, they will come" despite the fact that the phrase from the film is actually "If you build it, *he* will come.")

The phrase "Field of Dreams" has had a similar extended life. The 1994 book *Field of Screams* details accounts of baseball mayhem, and the 1998 book *Field of Schemes* attacks the propriety of public funding for stadium construction. The magazine *Nature Conservancy* decorated the cover of a 2001 edition with a beautiful photograph of farm land and the words, "Fields of Dreams Restoring Natural Landscapes." Visitors to the towns of Lewisburg, Pennsylvania, and Dade City, Florida, can now drive down Field of Dreams Lane in new housing developments courtesy of developers who also happen to be baseball fans.

Perhaps more impressive, an image established in *Field of Dreams* has become part of the national subconscious. As America endured the awful news that unfolded on September 11, 2001, as terrorist-hijacked airplanes struck the twin towers of the World Trade Center and the Pentagon, at least one man's thoughts were inspired by the film. When Jim Ogonowski addressed the press to speak about his brother John, the pilot of one of the planes that struck one of the World Trade Center towers in New York City, Jim reflected on his loss. Standing on a Massachusetts farm, Ogonowski said that he was still struggling to cope with his loss and hoping that his brother would walk out of the cornfield. The image from film, of departed ballplayers emerging from an Iowa cornfield, has become a collectively recognized synonym for a vision of heaven or the afterlife.

SYNCHRONICITIES, FELLOWSHIP, AND ISOLATION

The success of the images and phrases from the film and novel can be attributed to the skill of cinematographers or writers, but some find the coincidences that surround the proliferation of Field of Dreams references and linkages too eerie to be merely incidental. Synchronicities in the film *Field of Dreams*, like a husband and wife sharing a common dream about Fenway Park, help convince Ray Kinsella to follow the urgings of the voice and achieve ultimate reconciliation. Many people believe that similar synchronicities in their lives can help point them in the right direction. A simple coincidence may have no ability to predict the future. But, just as effective art does not have to be beautiful so long as it makes people think, synchronicities are significant if they cause people to pause from their daily routine to ponder some larger significance in their lives.

It is probably no surprise that people who were inspired by the words used to promote the film *Field of Dreams*—"If you believe the impossible, the incredible can come true"—see the coincidences of life as a call to action. Frequent field visitor Nancy Caruso went so far as to declare that those synchronicities are "signs of God's presence."

After seeing the film, many viewers decided the story was meant for them. Concluding that receiving that message was more than just coincidence, they decide they must travel to Iowa to express themselves to their loved ones. But the trip to the Field of Dreams is more than an attempt to connect one to one. It is a fashioning of a community.

Bartlett Giamatti sums up the ability of sports to create fellowship in *Take Time for Paradise*, suggesting, "Very soon the crowd is no crowd at all but a community, a small town of people sharing neither work nor pain nor deprivation nor anger but the common experience of being released to enjoy the moment, even those moments of intense disappointment or defeat, moments made better, after all, precisely because our fan is part of large family of those similarly affected, part of a city of grievers."

At the Field of Dreams, visitors open up to strangers and talk of matters they won't even share with family. Immersed in a kind of brotherhood of kindred spirits, they can speak in a common tongue. People who arrive as individuals or in small groups find themselves joining in the ongoing pickup game or engaging in a catch with someone they have just met. The expanding connection grows beyond the baseball, beyond the film and the field, until visitors become friends bonded by a unique association. Many visitors talk of the people they met for the first time in Dyersville who have become close friends. Some now exchange long-distance phone calls, e-mails, or Christmas cards.

The fellowship surrounding the Field of Dreams runs against societal trends that have eroded bonds between people and isolated individuals. In his much-discussed 2000 book *Bowling Alone*, Harvard University political science professor Robert D. Putnam argues that in recent years, dramatic technological advances, social changes, and economic shifts have "rendered obsolete" the set of bonds that have traditionally connected individuals and communities across America. In the analysis that gives the book its name, Putnam notes that even though Americans are bowling more than ever, they are not bowling in leagues—they are not joining together in organized groups to engage in the activity.

Putnam warns that the trends could be damaging to individuals, neighborhoods, and the nation as a whole, but the former youth bowling team member also suggested some hopeful findings. Commenting that America responded to a similar decline in social involvement a century ago with a renewed spirit of civic engagement resulting in institutions like the Boy Scouts, the League of Women Voters, and the Rotary, Putnam concluded with the hope that a similar resurgence could occur in the twenty-first century.

People find their place in the world by relating to those around them. They long to be part of a group and suffer when isolated. Even in an age of technological miracles where people around the globe can cocoon themselves in their homes and have nearly all their needs satisfied without any contact with another individual, no one can live with virtual relationships alone. Individuals' attempts to find satisfaction by moving away from others and choosing a private realm over a public realm are similarly fallacious.

SOMETHING FOR EVERYONE?

If the phenomenon surrounding the pilgrimage to the Field of Dreams is an indication of a communal spirit, it is not necessarily all-inclusive. By definition, creating a group inevitably omits those who are not in that group. Despite the praise heaped on the site for its ability to bring people together, some feel left out.

Many politicians have visited the Field of Dreams to use the charm of the unique attraction to underscore a campaign theme or to use imagery inspired from the film to illustrate their message. When former presidential candidate and conservative pundit Pat Buchanan visited the field for a campaign appearance, he said that it reminded him of the good old days of the 1950s and promised to give American kids the kind of country he enjoyed growing up during that era. Not everyone has the same happy memories of those old days.

Like the ballplayers who emerged from the corn, most of the visitors to the Field of Dreams are white. Some have questioned whether the nostalgia visitors seek is of a time that was simpler because it was uncomplicated by questions concerning sharing power and privilege with others who did not look like the majority. Thus, nonwhites and women—whether feeling excluded or absent because they do not see the message as speaking to them—are often underrepresented among Dyersville's visitors.

Kent Nelson reflected on the fact that, for his first trip to the Field of Dreams, he did not invite his mother, sisters, or wife. In retrospect, he was not so sure that the males-only trip was totally appropriate. His mother probably agreed. Kent recalled that his mother chided him as she wished him bon voyage. He said, "She wrote me a little note telling me she was proud of me for following my heart and getting a little emotional about things, and she said 'You little fart, I also hit you a lot of fly balls.'"

After reminding Kent that in the Nelson family it was clearly not just fathers playing catch with sons, she told him, "I'm proud of you. Go with your heart, go with your dreams, and have a great trip." Perhaps as a way of confessing that he should have included her on his journey, Kent bought her a jewelry box for Mother's Day engraved "Thanks for hitting me all those fly balls."

THE FUTURE OF THE FIELD OF DREAMS

Years after *Field of Dreams* appeared in theaters, the film still plays on television and remains on the shelves of video stores. *Shoeless Joe* can still be found in bookstores. With its ability to connect on many levels with many different audiences—as a reminder of a popular film, as a representation of a simple way of life, as a location that offers the promise of spiritual in the secular world, as a site where redemption and the power of second chances are real, and as a vestige linked to the romantic aspects of baseball—the Field of Dreams crosses demographic and socioeconomic barriers and demonstrates widespread appeal.

Certainly the inspiration for the visit to Dyersville could stay in the popular culture, but what of the attractiveness of a simple place, the search for the sacred in the secular world, or the need for a catalyst to bring generations together? Will it still have a pull for future generations, or are aging baby boomers and children of the sixties the only ones who will react to this attraction? Will the field's allure endure?

If the stream of visitors continues, a more salient question could concern the stewardship of the attraction itself. Given the Field's divided ownership and the tension surrounding how the site should be interpreted for visitors, one must wonder how the parties involved will continue to make the attraction work. Although the site is still privately owned by two families who pledge to maintain the former movie set, one cannot be certain how the passage of time will affect the attraction or how visitors will find the Field of Dreams a quarter century from today.

Al Vigil, who heads the limited-liability corporation that leased the Ameskamps' portion of the Field of Dreams and now runs Left and Center Field of Dreams, remembered his first impression of the field and his vision for its future. "It was five years ago on our wedding anniversary that we actually accidentally came upon the field, and it was the first time that I'd ever seen grown men play with young kids and have such a great time, so I thought it was fabulous," he said. "The ideal situation is that someone would come in and buy the entire field, take that and turn it over to a foundation and then that foundation would own it so that the field was here forever—and it belongs to the people."

Many would love to see the field become something more—some would advocate holding regular games on the diamond; others would have more events to expand tourism's impact; others would preserve it as a special camp for the underprivileged or for youth with disabilities. The families who own the land of the unlikely attraction are less certain about what the future of the Field of Dreams should be. Neither the Ameskamps nor the Lansings asked to play host for this phenomenon, and the Field of Dreams was never meant to be a tourist attraction. But, given the opportunity and responsibility to host the hundreds of thousands of visitors who have traveled to Dyersville in recent years, they have responded well, sharing their gift with the world and preserving their bequest for posterity.

Kent Nelson, for one, was happy that the Iowa farmers have been so accepting of visitors. "I so appreciate the interest and the efforts that Don Lansing has gone to allow people to continue to enjoy a spot of his, and the other family as well," he said. "This can't have all been good, but I appreciate his willingness to perhaps look at the big picture and understand that there are probably hundreds and hundreds and hundreds of thousands of stories that have been written, could be written, and many more yet to come, but I am so appreciative of him allowing us to trod on that earth, and I'm so very thankful for having had that chance growing up to play ball with my father."

Because of the unique set of motivations that bring visitors to Dyersville, the hosts are almost like priests or doctors, privy to visitors' innermost thoughts and entrusted with their secrets. Despite the fact that they have no formal training or expressed desire to fill the role, they have been granted the responsibility to safeguard stories of happiness and tragedy and have become custodians of a particular slice of Americana and one representation of the American dream.

Some visitors have even been dismayed when they discovered that the farmers who received them at the Field of Dreams had no special knowledge to impart and could offer little to solve the mysteries of life that they came to the field trying to answer. Happily, most visitors are content just to be received hospitably by down-to-earth people who are glad to tend their land and smile with wonder that people continue to arrive at their doorsteps.

Both the Lansings and the Ameskamps have tended the Field of Dreams with care. Farmers nurture what sprouts in their fields and put their heart into their work to make something grow. It is true that the Lansings and Ameskamps have differed about how to present the Field of Dreams to visitors, but only at the margins. While they may have disagreed about hours of operations, the appearance of the Ghost Players, or the recent addition of a corn maze, they have managed to agree (actively or tacitly) on most details. There are no roller coasters through the corn or special-effects technology where visitors can act in a scene from the film so that they can carry home a video of themselves as Ray Kinsella. In general, the field looks as people who watched the film think it would look, and pictures taken on the field look like stills from the film except for the presence of a few additional "extras" posing for their friends. The magic of walking onto the field as if one is a visitor arriving the day after the film ends remains enchanting.

Al Ameskamp definitively stated, "All I want to see out of this is people having fun."

"And leaving happy," Rita Ameskamp added.

The Lansings have expressed similar sentiments. Even though tensions between the owners have led to disagreements, the fact that ownership and stewardship are shared has also prevented either from doing anything to totally change the way the place works. The field continues to exist pretty much unchanged since its creation. That may not have been the case if one person or group totally owned it and one opinion or way of viewing it had total sway.

Looking forward, the lack of a singular long-range strategy does not interfere with the experience for visitors. In his essay "The Magic Cocktail: The Enduring Appeal of the 'Field of Dreams,'" Hamilton College English professor Bobby Fong notes, "The farm in Dyersville is under no threat of foreclosure, and the owner welcomes travelers to the 'Field of Dreams' to use the diamond free of charge. This is as it should be, for dreams and imagination and memories and love are without price. Kinsella and Robinson and *Shoeless Joe* and *Field of Dreams* were prophetically right: If you build it, people will come."

IS THERE MAGIC IN THE CORN?

Kent Nelson certainly found magic in the corn. "The Field of Dreams provided for me a venue in which I can rekindle a lost magic," he remembered. "It's funny. Now I think I can do something similar in other places easier for having that delightful experience in Dyersville, and I don't believe that it would be that easy to do if I hadn't been there. But I think the magic is in all of us. It's just a mecca, if you will, or a spot to which people make pilgrimages that perhaps allowed us to go ahead and strip away and expose our youth and get reenthused about what we held to be important and almost sacred, and I think that that cornfield in Iowa made that magic reappear easier than I could have done it without it."

After filming *Field of Dreams,* Phil Alden Robinson questioned whether such emotions require the catalyst of the field to be released. "I salute the people who go out there and have some emotional cathartic experience, and if that's what it takes, then it's a wonderful thing," he said. "Personally, I just think that it would be something nice if, eventually, that were a cornfield again because this field is about dreams; it's about the imagination. It's not about the actual dirt and the actual sod that's laid there; it's about what you bring to it in your own imagination. You don't have go to Iowa to connect with this. You can have a catch with your son or your father on your own front yard. That's exactly the same."

But when told of the number of visitors the field continues to attract, Robinson's reaction marginally changed. "I think its lovely," he said. "I don't think that you have to travel to Iowa to do that, but if someone feels that they do, if that's what gives them the context in which to do this, fine. I think it's a wonderful thing for a film to do."

Actor Timothy Busfield had a similar shift in his view of the Field of Dreams phenomenon. After filming, he said, "Whatever is in your own back yard, you don't need to go looking for all these dreams in your own life. It's probably in your own back yard. It's simpler than you think."

But after spending some time in Dyersville observing the visitors for himself, Busfield reflected on the ongoing pilgrimage. "I can't describe it in any other way other than it's what people cherish. There is something in that field for them which speaks to them, and I don't know why. I still don't know why, but it's truly a magical experience for them."

Field of Dreams executive producer Brian Frankish takes pride in the power of the film he helped bring to life and the location he helped select as the site for the *Field of Dreams.* "This is a motion picture that changed people's lives," he said. "It was such a magical experience actually making the motion picture that anything that happens to anybody going there later pales in comparison to the reality."

But is magic really the appeal? Even the most ardent fans of illusionists and magicians do not really believe that the show they see on stage is anything more than a remarkable trick, skillfully performed. If there is magic, it is in the audience members' ability to suspend their collective disbelief to enjoy the performance without complaining that they are being deceived with sleight of hand. Maybe the magic is not in anything that actually occurs as part of a performance but in the fact that the audience plays along. Similarly, the collective search for the extraordinary often takes people in a number of directions far and wide while they remain unable to notice the magic before them.

It may be overly sentimental to say that there is a little Field of Dreams in everyone, but it is clear that everyone has the capacity to seek redemption, to forgive, and to find a deeper meaning in a secular world. There may be no magic in the site itself, but there is magic in people's hearts and maybe it takes something like the Field of Dreams to draw it out.

Langston Hughes wondered what happens to a dream deferred. He pondered whether it dries up like a raisin in the sun or festers like a sore. If a dream is deferred, Hughes asked, does it sag like a heavy load—or does it explode? Perhaps the most significant power of the Field of Dreams is its ability is to prevent dreams from being deferred or, conversely, to allow dreams to be realized. If that is the case, then maybe the field is not a field of dreams at all but a field of realities and abilities. After all, if you build it and if you will it, it is no longer a dream.

In 1870, future lawyer, preacher, author, and Temple University founder Russell Conwell visited the Middle East, where a guide entertained his traveling party with a legend of a wealthy Persian farmer. Although the farmer, Al Hafed, was content, his life changed when a visiting Buddhist priest told him about the magnificence of diamonds. Al Hafed was suddenly discontented and set off on a journey that took him far and wide until all his money was spent and the once-prosperous farmer was in rags and poverty. So distraught was Al Hafed that he cast

himself into the sea and drowned. But while Al Hafed's quest was unsuccessful, his successor found a bounty of diamonds on the lands Al Hafed
left. Had Al Hafed remained at home, he would have avoided poverty
and death, and he would have found acres of diamonds.

Years after hearing the story of Al Hafed, Conwell incorporated
the tale into his famous "Acres of Diamonds" lecture, a message of
optimism he delivered thousands of times for millions of listeners. To
Conwell, the message of Al Hafed's tale was "Your diamonds are not in
far-away mountains or in distant seas; they are in your own back yard
if you will but dig for them."

Conwell's oft-repeated declaration is a warning to everyone. One
should not wander to seek out happiness or search for diamonds—in
cornfields or elsewhere. One should endeavor to do what is necessary
to find that happiness and those diamonds at home.

Is the *Field of Dreams* movie site heaven? The site is certainly special,
but it is not truly holy. Is there magic in the corn? There is definitely
something about the Iowa setting that inspires visitors, but the corn is
just corn, and any magic found there probably arrived in the hearts of
those who visit. Is it a place where dreams can come true? Visitors can
certainly make dreams come true in Dyersville, but only if the desire to
make something happen travels with them to Iowa.

Just before the climactic fatherson reconciliation at the end of *Field
of Dreams*, Ray Kinsella finally makes sense of the messages the voice
has been sending him. "Shoeless" Joe Jackson repeats the words of the
voice, "If you build it, he will come," and then Kinsella sees his father.

"Ease his pain," Ray says.

"Go the distance," Annie adds.

Realizing what is occurring, Ray looks toward his father and utters,
"It was you."

"No, Ray, it was you," responds the ghostly Jackson before disappearing.

Just as Ray finally realizes that the messages did not have the meanings he originally attributed to them—the messages were about himself,

not his father or "Shoeless" Joe Jackson—the question about the power of the Dyersville's field could be misdirected. The movie-set-turned-pop-culture-mecca is not heaven, but those who travel to the Field of Dreams do not necessarily need to find heaven in the Iowa corn. They find it in themselves when they look for it.

The magic of the Field of Dreams is almost certainly not in the location itself or the setting amid the Iowa corn but in the faith visitors bring to Dyersville and in the memories they take home with them. That faith and those memories have encouraged hundreds of thousands of visitors to make the trip over the course of a single decade.

The pilgrimage to the Field of Dreams movie site started in fantasy at the end of the film as a line of cars stretching from the Kinsella farm all the way to the horizon. In reality, people like Jim Bohn, Mark Babiarz, and countless others continue the stream of visitors to Dyersville and find that the magic of the Field of Dreams is truly heavenly.

Afterword

Aloysius "Al" Ameskamp died on June 18, 2001, after a long battle with cancer. He was sixty-five. In addition to wife Rita, Al was survived by four children and six grandchildren. As Rita recalled, "Al loved maintaining the field and loved to watch the joy and enthusiasm of the people that came to visit the field."

On the night before he passed, he received a call from Kevin Costner. While Al was not well, Rita put the receiver to his ear so he could hear from the actor who once spoke his lines on Al's land. Al could not respond but was able to listen as Costner paid his respects—a final connection to the film that helped attract the world to his doorstep. Ameskamp's memorial card featured a picture of the Field of Dreams full of visitors on a sunny afternoon and the word *Memories* rising from the acres of farmland into the clear blue sky. After services in the Basilica of St. Francis Xavier, Al was interred in a Dyersville cemetery just a short drive from the Field of Dreams.

2020 Update:
A Whole New Ballgame

Three decades after moviegoers first saw *Field of Dreams* in theaters, Major League Baseball and local officials surprised film lovers and baseball fans alike by declaring that, indeed, "people will come." Announcing that Major League Baseball would host an official regular-season game on a diamond to be built in the cornfields just a short fly ball from the Field of Dreams Movie Site, Baseball Commissioner Robert Manfred, Jr. proudly noted that life would imitate art in the celebrated Iowa cornfield. "As a sport that is proud of its history linking generations, Major League Baseball is excited to bring a regular season game to the site of *Field of Dreams*," he proclaimed. "We look forward to celebrating the movie's enduring message of how baseball brings people together at this special cornfield in Iowa."

So it was set that a little more than thirty years after fictionalized major leaguers Shoeless Joe Jackson and Archibald "Moonlight" Graham took to the field among the rows of Dyersville corn on the silver screen, real major leaguers would come out of the Iowa corn to play a regular-season game. With the eyes of the baseball world trained on Iowa (watching the game instead of welling with tears), the years of pilgrimages to the Field of Dreams Movie Site reached an unlikely pinnacle.

In the film *Field of Dreams*, fictional Terrence Mann prophesied that people would happily pass over $20 to "find they have reserved seats somewhere along one of the baselines, where they sat when they were children and cheered their heroes." Of course, tickets to see real Major League Baseball in Iowa were a bit more expensive, but fans were happy to pay big-league ticket prices to be among the intimate crowd for the unique event.

Transforming the cornfields into a film set was a tremendous undertaking. Creating a Major-League-Baseball-worthy ballpark was an even more ambitious project. Enduring the uncertainty when the coronavirus pandemic upended the 2020 season (and ultimately led to a postponement of the Field of Dreams Game) was a test of faith for everyone who believed in the magic in the Iowa corn. Learning that the game at the Field of Dreams Movie Site would occur in 2021 was just what baseball fans needed to remind them "of all that once was good, and that could be again."

The book *Is This Heaven? The Magic of the Field of Dreams* was first published in 2002. Nearly two decades later, visitors still find the Field of Dreams Movie Site as if they were among the first in the continuous line of cars that snaked to the field in the scene just before the credits rolled. Since this book's first publication, a few things have changed.

Six years after the death of Al Ameskamp, Rita Ameskamp sold her family's land, including the left- and center-field portions of the Field of Dreams to Don and Becky Lansing. The sale ended the sometimes contentious divide between the two families that fate and circumstance made stewards of this unique tourist attraction and cultural touchstone. When the field was divided, the "Left and Center Field of Dreams" ownership was generally open to the idea of commercialized events and gimmicks to attract and entertain visitors while the owners of the "Field of Dreams Movie Site" were cool to the idea of doing much more than allowing visitors to experience the field as they had seen it in the film.

In 2006, for example, as part of a Netflix-sponsored promotion highlighting famous films and their locales, Kevin Costner and his band *Modern West* played a concert at the Field of Dreams before an on-field screening of the film. More properly, the event was hosted in the left- and center-field portion of the field as the lingering disagreements between the co-owners kept such events off the Lansing-owned portion of the site. Similarly, the Ghost Players restricted their regular appearances at the field to the outfield grass. Once the field was under the exclusive control of the Lansing family, those commercialized events were discontinued.

After the original publication of this book, I visited Dyersville as part of a modest book tour. My book signings were slightly awkward as the ownership of the attraction was still shared between the two families and I signed books at the Left and Center Field of Dreams gift shop on one day and then at the Field of Dreams Movie Site gift shop the next. The experience was a lot like so many holidays I spent shuttling between families after my parents' divorce. Still, it was great fun to meet so many people who were eager to read stories of the field and its pull. Many had their own charming, moving, and even heart-wrenching reasons for making a visit. I brought my father on the trip and found it meaningful to have our own catch and long conversations on the Field of Dreams. The tens of thousands of visitors each year that continued to make their own trips to the site seemingly agreed.

The Lansings' exclusive ownership of the Field of Dreams was short-lived. In 2010, Don and Becky surprised locals and *Field of Dreams* lovers by announcing that they were putting the famous movie site, along with the Lansing homestead and acres of Iowa farmland that had been owned by the family for more than a century, up for sale. Somehow fittingly, the real estate consultant overseeing the transaction was a former major-league pitcher. "It's really time for us to head to the locker room," Becky said to a reporter at the time. "Maybe that sounds corny. I don't care. We really would just love to become spectators. We want to sit in the bleachers. We want to look forward to all that the Field of Dreams will become in the future."

At the same time, in suburban Chicago, marketing professional and travel-baseball mom Denise Stillman saw a unique opportunity.

A successful entrepreneur and fundraiser, Stillman self-published the 2011 book, *Courageous Clarity: Four Keys to Unlock the Leader Inside*, which offered a quartet of inspirational maxims that drove her personal and professional philosophy: "Congruence—live a life that is true to the real self; Aspiration—engage the human capacity to dream; Intent—begin with the end in mind; Action—discipline the self to build toward dreams."

Stillman believed that the Field of Dreams could not only be a connection to a movie about baseball's past, but an important link to baseball's future, conceiving a new dream for the Dyersville movie site. She saw the Midwest as underserved in the lucrative youth-baseball-tournament marketplace that attracts teams from across the country to multi-field complexes near the National Baseball Hall of Fame in Cooperstown and other coastal locations. Stillman sought to create "All-Star Ballpark Heaven," a complex that would include two dozen baseball diamonds, a minor-league ballpark, an indoor training facility, player dorms, and a conference center. The Field of Dreams Movie Site itself would remain unchanged and open to the public to be enjoyed as it had been since the credits first rolled. Just a short stroll through the cornfields that produced on-screen magic, the new slice of baseball heaven would await.

Stillman formed a corporation that included baseball Hall of Fame legend Wade Boggs and *Friends* actor Matthew Perry among other local and far-flung investors. In 2012, their company, "Go the Distance Baseball," purchased the Field of Dreams Movie Site and nearly 200 acres of Iowa corn fields for $3.4 million, paying a per-acre price that was more than twice the average farmland value for Dubuque County at the time. Of course, the Lansing land produced tourists as well as feed corn.

The All-Star Ballpark Heaven proposal also produced some controversy. Dyersville's mayor and other local leaders were active supporters of the project with its potential to bring new vitality to the allure of the Field of Dreams (along with the promise of tens of millions of dollars in outside investment and the creation of dozens of seasonal and year-round jobs). A vocal group of local and remote opponents protested. Concerns about the increased traffic, noise, and light that the new development would bring troubled many locals, including Al and Rita Ameskamp's son, who spoke out against the proposal. Worries about the preservation of the pop-culture holy site concerned certain fans. One national magazine's story about the clashes asked the question, "Should the field's fake authenticity be preserved?" and recounted a column published in an Iowa newspaper that "expressed concern that the development would facilitate the area's 'Disneyfi-cation.'" Worries about traffic or other negative impacts from additional visitors to Dyersville was certainly understandable. But the local pushback over the potential "Disneyfication" of the site was, perhaps, a little alarmist given the fact that the pop-culture mecca was always pop-culture before it was an actual holy site. Life and art continued to mix wonderfully and sometimes not so easily at the unique attraction.

After months of meetings and protests and lawsuits and discussions, the All-Star Ballpark Heaven proposal finally secured the necessary governmental approvals and legal sanctions to move forward. Disputes over the project had taken their toll in a number of ways. Dyersville's mayor and the city council members up for reelection were defeated at the polls in the aftermath of the controversies. Fund-raising efforts and planning work for All-Star Ballpark Heaven slowed. Some enthusiasts wondered if the controversy left the Field of Dreams with just a little less magic.

The All-Star Ballpark Heaven proposal may have generated squabbling, but the *Field of Dreams* movie continued to move visitors to journey to the former Lansing farm. When the Field of Dreams Movie Site celebrated its silver anniversary, a quarter-century after the film's release, it was clear that the connections that made a visit to the field so special endured.

In 2014, to commemorate the twenty-fifth anniversary, the Field of Dreams Movie Site hosted a celebration over Father's Day Weekend.

Field of Dreams stars Kevin Costner, Timothy Busfield, and Dwier Brown made the trip to Dyersville along with thousands of fans from near and far to commemorate the milestone. An estimated 12,000 fans enjoyed activities including an on-field screening of the film, a round-table discussion with the actors hosted by broadcaster Bob Costas, and a celebrity ballgame that packed the bleachers with cheering fans. The Ghost Players, welcomed back to perform their greatest show on dirt under the new ownership group, entertained the crowd. Generations of fans choked the field itself to enjoy a simple game of catch on a brilliant sunny day.

I brought my own son with me to Iowa in 2014 and was tickled to play catch at the site with him. We joined the crowd on the field to watch a screening of the movie, which felt slightly like being in an M. C. Escher drawing or looking at the endless reflections in a hall of mirrors. The following day, I participated in the celebrity game on the field. Kevin Costner's team, including actor Dwier Brown, broadcaster Bob Costas, and former Royals ace Bret Saberhagen, defeated Timothy Busfield's team, which included former major-league pitcher Glendon Rusch, and this author. A few thousand fans enjoyed the ballgame, cheering the stars and celebrating the film that spawned the continuing pilgrimage. "A lot of times people go, 'You know, the movies . . . movies don't mean anything,'" Costner said at the event of the staying power of the film and the site. "This one did. This little movie did."

Dwier Brown, who played John Kinsella and had an on-screen catch on the field with Kevin Costner as Ray Kinsella, wrote and published the book, *If You Build It . . .* that same year. The book, about Brown's experiences with the film and interactions with individuals moved by its message, was cathartic for the actor who had lost his own father just before filming began for *Field of Dreams*. For the actor/author, the connection to the film and the emotions it inspires remained a large part of the attraction's allure. "In the two-and-a-half decades since *Field of Dreams* was released in 1989, dozens of people have come up to me to tell me how seeing the movie has affected their lives and to share a story about their father or their daughter or their son," he wrote. "I try to absorb every word and soak up every nuance, as if it were my father talking to me again about important things, the things that hurt him and the things that made him happy."

The film *Field of Dreams* is about second chances, regrets, and dreams. It is also about death and reflecting on lives lived and the choices people make along the way.

Shoeless Joe author W. P. Kinsella died in 2016. The author suffered a head injury after being struck by a car as a pedestrian in 1997 and lost his senses of smell and taste along with the focus required to write. As a result, the formerly prolific author did not publish another novel until 2011's *Butterfly Winter*, a final magical-reality story involving baseball and twins who enjoy their first catch in the womb. Especially in his later years, the author developed a reputation for cantankerousness, but he was responsive whenever I reached out to him. He declined to be interviewed for this book in 2001, politely but cryptically emailing, "I don't think I want to cooperate on a project that I intend to pursue in the future." As far as I know, he never did any writing about the phenomenon he inspired. I last heard from him in 2014 after I visited the Field of Dreams Movie Site to participate in the twenty-fifth anniversary festivities. He responded to my email about the event, "Was not there. Not invited." That was the last time I heard from him. Kinsella was eighty-one when he died.

Denise Stillman was only forty-six when she passed. The visionary and energetic force behind Go The Distance Baseball and All-Star Ballpark Heaven succumbed to a very rare and aggressive form of cancer on November 7, 2018. Just a year and a half after her diagnosis, she was gone. Under Stillman's stewardship, the Field of Dreams Movie Site was preserved, polished, and presented in novel ways to generations of fans. Through her efforts, the Field of Dreams hosted events like the twenty-fifth anniversary celebration, the return of an annual Labor Day "Team of Dreams" game featuring celebrities and baseball legends, and monthly "Ghost Sunday" performances by the Ghost Players.

While the field remains open for quiet contemplation, it is also open for business. From matchups featuring local teams to senior-league baseball tournaments, the field is now often booked for games. Democratic presidential candidate and Vermont Senator Bernie Sanders brought his 2020 presidential campaign to the Field of Dreams Movie Site for a ballgame, after which campaign donors received baseball cards that memorialized the effort to woo Iowa Caucus participants.

Visitors who want to truly "go the distance" can now enjoy a very special sleepover at the movie site. The old Lansing farmhouse (or Kinsella homestead if one prefers) can be rented Airbnb-style for those who want to gaze at the field from the bay window like the fictional Kinsella family—or look for ghosts like Moonlight Graham under moonlight when other tourists are gone. At $900 per night for a peak-season, weekend night stay, the booking is not for everyone, but those who can afford it can truly live as if they were part of the film.

One estimate suggested that the number of annual visitors to the field had fallen to 65,000 before Stillman and her group purchased the Lansing land. In 2018, about 115,000 visitors made the trip. According to Roman Weinberg, operations manager for the Field of Dreams Movie Site, the field still, "speaks to people and draws on memories they have from growing up—not only of baseball, but of loved ones." Greeting thousands of visitors each year, Weinberg sees the field as a place where people can "forget about their trials and tribulations and just dream."

Stillman's dream for All-Star Ballpark Heaven endures, as well as her vision to build a connection between the movie about baseball's past and the ballplayers of baseball's future in the cornfields surrounding the Field of Dreams Movie Site. Plans to build a tournament site, training facility, and hospitality center have been redrawn to fit an evolving scope for the overall project. A future where youth-baseball tournaments, training for future major leaguers, and weddings are hosted on site may come to fruition in the coming years.

Just weeks after celebrations for the *Field of Dreams* film's thirtieth anniversary in 2019 focused renewed attention on the Field of Dreams Movie Site, Major League Baseball made the remarkable announcement that it would come to Dyersville. Suddenly, the Field of Dreams was not just a set from a classic modern film slowly fading into history, but a setting for modern baseball history.

Under Commissioner Manfred, Major League Baseball has shown some outside-the-batter's-box thinking in hosting sanctioned, regular-season games in nontraditional venues. In recent years, major-league teams have played games on an active military base in North Carolina; in a minor-league stadium in Williamsport, Pennsylvania, as part of a celebration of the Little League World Series; in an Omaha, Nebraska ballpark to kick off the College World Series; and across the Atlantic Ocean in a London football (soccer) stadium to spread the reach of the big-league game.

Still, it was a shock to baseball fans, film lovers, and dreamers everywhere when, on August 8, 2019, Major League Baseball and Iowa officials announced that construction would begin on a temporary 8,000-seat ballpark at the Field of Dreams Movie Site to host the first major-league game in the Hawkeye State. (True fans of the writings of W. P. Kinsella might quibble that the Chicago Cubs played a game against players from the Iowa Baseball Confederacy in the town of Big Inning, Iowa, in 1908—at least that is how the protagonist of Kinsella's *The Iowa Baseball Confederacy* remembers it.)

Major League Baseball had leaned upon imagery and memories from *Field of Dreams* to promote its product before. Big-league stars recited lines from Terrence Mann's "People Will Come" speech for a video promoting 2015's Opening Week and MLB Network's introduction for the 2013 playoffs used editing magic to show modern players "in action" on the Field of Dreams while Ray Liotta narrated a sentimental introduction. But real big-league baseball at the Field of Dreams would be a whole new ballgame.

Major League Baseball and its partners worked to ensure that fans in the ballpark and viewers across the globe would enjoy a first-class spectacle. While the fictional Ray Kinsella toiled mostly alone to turn his rows of corn into a ballfield on the silver screen, a group of companies with experience creating temporary sports facilities were selected to bring the vision to reality (and to address the logistical challenges necessary to bring thousands of attendees to the off-the-beaten-path locale). Everything from the major-league worthy field itself, to showers and clubhouses for the players, restrooms and souvenir stands for fans, and press boxes for media representatives covering the game had to be constructed "like a giant Lego set" on site—all with an eye toward creating the feel of a major-league game while preserving the Field of Dreams' unique sense of place.

The setting for the Major League Baseball game took shape a short walk from the outfield of the Field of Dreams. A pathway cut through the iconic fields of corn to lead fans to the ballpark. The shape of the outfield and bullpens behind the center-field wall paid homage to Chicago's Comiskey Park, which closed one year after the film *Field of Dreams* debuted in theaters. The right-field wall was constructed with windows so players and fans could see the cornfields beyond the home-run fence. Unspoiled views of a gorgeous Iowa summer sunset, along with the aroma of pig manure carried by the breeze provided the final bits of local authenticity.

As plans for the event came together slowly over years of conversations, the most unlikely aspect of the event might have been that it remained a well-kept secret for so long. NBC Universal, which owns the rights to *Field of Dreams*, was involved in supporting the idea, along with Iowa and Dyersville officials, team executives, contractors and consultants, and personnel at the Field of Dreams Movie Site. All involved managed to keep the exciting news quiet while plans were finalized and approvals were secured. But once the story broke, it created a sensation that crossed over sports and entertainment news and captured the imagination of social-media users. FOX announced that the game would be broadcast live (a rarity for a regular-season, mid-week matchup) so millions of fans across the globe could enjoy the game.

In anticipation of the increased attention on the former film set, the premium off-the-field baseball brand, Baseballism (sellers of a popular t-shirt featuring a silhouette of the State of Iowa with the words "IS THIS HEAVEN?") announced it would establish a retail store on the Field of Dreams Movie Site. The new store, designed as a retrofitted barn, would replace the existing gift shop in time for the surge of visitors for the game. With the unique partnership, the baseball-lifestyle retailer and pop-culture touchstone took the Field of Dreams souvenir-stand game to a big-league level to greet new throngs of visitors.

The original proposals for All-Star Ballpark Heaven included building a small ballpark to host a Minor League Baseball franchise near the Field of Dreams Movie Site. There was nothing minor about the plans for the Major League game. Denise Stillman and Major League Baseball officials began discussions about the idea of a big-league game in Dyersville in 2015. With Baseball Commissioner Manfred exploring ways to promote the game outside of the footprint of current major-league media markets, the idea to host a game amidst the Iowa corn took root and then became real.

Denise Stillman died before the plans were made official, but her colleagues say she died believing that the Major League game at the Field of Dreams would happen and that it would help realize her dream of building All-Star Baseball Heaven. The plan to host big leaguers for a single game anticipated that the temporary ballpark bleachers, lights, and structural elements would vanish like the players walking into the corn in *Field of Dreams* shortly after the game. But the second baseball diamond carved into the Dyersville corn fields will remain. Future Field of Dreams Movie Site visitors will be able to see the field where fictional baseball history was set as well as see the field where actual baseball history occurred. In the near future, the cornfields surrounding the former movie set and former major-league field will continue to be leased to local farmers to grow their crops, but—if the vision of Go the

Distance Baseball is realized—the answer to the question of what's out there in the corn might someday be: All-Star Baseball Heaven.

Three decades after moviemakers transformed the Lansing farm into a Hollywood back lot, film lovers and families still find their way to the unlikely attraction. Looking for a connection with memories of a favorite film or searching for redemption in the Iowa corn, visitors now span new generations. Grandparents and fathers and mothers who all saw the film in theaters, and their children who watched the film on VHS tapes and DVDs—and now their children's children who have streamed *Field of Dreams* online—have all made the trip. Former baseball greats, politicians, and celebrities have played in exhibition matches at the field. But with the remarkable decision to host an actual Major League Baseball game in Dyersville, this fictional location was finally able to host real baseball history. The words, "people will most definitely come" continue to prove more true than a Canadian author or a Hollywood screenwriter could have ever imagined.

Notes

Chapter 1 Notes

Much of the material in this chapter is based on my research in Dyersville and at the Field of Dreams; go to fieldofdreamsmoviesite.com and www.leftandcenterfod.com for a virtual visit. The comments from Jim Bohn come from an interview conducted by telephone in fall 2000. Jim Bohn's letter to Don Lansing is quoted from Peter McWilliams's book *Life 101: Everything We Wish We Had Learned about Life in School—But Didn't (The Life 101 Series)* (Prelude Press, 1997) and confirmed by Bohn. Quotations from *Field of Dreams* are taken directly from the 1998 DVD version of the film. The Bob Puhala *Chicago Sun-Times* article, "Where the Real Baseball Lives," appeared on April 16, 1995. Some of the kind words for Dyersville come from information published by the Dyersville Area Chamber of Commerce. Visitor comments about the Field of Dreams were quoted directly from guest books at the Field of Dreams. The comments from Iowa Film Office manager Wendol Jarvis come from an interview conducted in person during summer 2000. While most of Phil Alden Robinson's comments were recorded during a telephone conversation in fall 2000, some material is quoted from the 1998 *Field of Dreams* DVD and the Field of Dreams Movie Site Official Souvenir Program (Low and Inside Creative, 1999). Sue Reidel's comments were recorded during a telephone conversation in fall 2000. Don Lansing's quotations were recorded during an interview conducted in person during summer 2000. Additional comments from Lansing come from the 1998 *Field of Dreams* DVD and from *Thanks for Going the Distance* (Low and Inside, 1992). Lansing's comments in the *New York Times* were published on June 11, 1989, in an article titled "Field of Reality." Al and Rita Ameskamp's comments were recorded during an interview conducted in person in summer 2000, with additional remarks quoted from the 1998 *Field of Dreams* DVD and *Thanks for Going the Distance*. Betty Boeckenstedt's quotations come from an interview conducted in person during summer 2000. Brian Frankish's quotations were recorded during a fall 2000 telephone conversation. While I interviewed Timothy Busfield in fall 2000 and James Earl Jones in summer 2000, their quotations in this chapter come from the 1998 *Field of Dreams* DVD. W. P. Kinsella's comments are also from the 1998 *Field of Dreams* DVD. Charles Fruehling Springwood's book *Cooperstown to Dyersville: A Geography of Baseball Nostalgia* was published in 1996.

Chapter 2 Notes

Sources for this chapter include comments from Becky Lansing taken from an interview conducted in person in summer 2000. The song about the "little brown church in the vale" is "The Church in the Wildwood" by Dr. William S. Pitts, written in 1857 and originally published in 1865. The letter about the *Field of Dreams* baseball was published in *Sports Collectors Digest* on January 26, 2001. Visitor comments about the Field of Dreams were quoted directly from guest books at the Field of Dreams. Faith Popcorn's concepts come from her 1997 book *Clicking*. The *Licensing Industry Survey 2000* was published by the International Licensing Industry Merchandisers' Association, New York. Statistics on notable television show viewership come from Neilsen Media Research. Estimates of the Starr Report's Internet traffic come from ZDNet. Quotations from *Field of Dreams* are taken directly from the 1998 DVD version of the film. Quotations from *Shoeless Joe* are taken directly from W. P. Kinsella's 1982 book. Phil Alden Robinson's comments were recorded during a telephone conversation in fall 2000. Additional Robinson material is quoted from the 1998 *Field of Dreams* DVD and from the May 1989 edition of *American Film*. Most of W. P. Kinsella's comments are from the 1998 *Field of Dreams* DVD, but his remarks about baseball come from the Field of Dreams Movie Site Official Souvenir Program (Low and Inside Creative, 1999) and from an August 15, 1989, *Philadelphia Inquirer* article titled "There's More to Kinsella's Literary Trove Than Baseball." Kinsella's comments on baseball writing appeared in the spring 1987 edition of *Modern Fiction Studies*. Kinsella's comments on proper charges for admittance to the Field of Dreams appeared in an article titled "A Battlefield of Dreams for Iowa Farmers," which appeared in the *New York Times* on August 6, 1999. George Plimpton's praise of *Shoeless Joe* comes from the paperback edition of the book, first published in 1983. Jack McCallum's "Reel Sports" article appeared in the February 5, 2001, issue of *Sports Illustrated*. Caryn James's review of *Field of Dreams* appeared in the *New York Times* ("A Baseball Diamond Becomes the Stuff of Dreams," April 21, 1989); Pauline Kael's review appeared in *The New Yorker* (May 1, 1989); Roger Angell's comments about the film appeared in *The New Yorker* (July 31, 1989). Reviews appeared in *Time* (April 24, 1989), *People Weekly* (May 15, 1989), *The New Republic* (May 8, 1989), *The Nation* (May 15, 1989), *Film Comment* (May/June 1989), *Rolling Stone* (May 18, 1989), *New York* (April 24, 1989), *Variety* (April 19, 1989), *Newsweek* (April 24, 1989), *Los Angeles Magazine* (May 1989), *National Catholic Reporter* (May 26, 1989), *Philadelphia Magazine,* (July 1989), *Playboy* (July 1989), *Maclean's,* (May 1, 1989), and *Cosmopolitan* (June 1989). Tom O'Brien's review in *Commonweal* appeared on May 19, 1989. Steve Wulf's review appeared in *Sports Illustrated* on May 1, 1989. W. P. Kinsella's review appeared in *Cineplus* (April 21–May 4, 1989). Brian Frankish's quotations were recorded during a fall 2000 telephone conversation. Timothy Busfield's comments also come from a fall 2000 telephone interview. James Earl Jones's comments were recorded during a summer 2000 telephone interview. Kevin Costner's comments about *Field of Dreams* are quoted from the Iowa Department of Economic Development's March 29, 1989, press release on the occasion of the world premiere of *Field of Dreams* and from *Premiere* (May 1989). Baseline, Inc., provided the statistics regarding the financial performance of the film *Field of Dreams.* Roger Ebert's comments are quoted from Ebert's online "Roger Ebert on Movies" website, www.suntimes.com/ebert/ebert_reviews/1989/04/349987.html. Don Lansing's quotations were recorded during an interview conducted in person during summer 2000. Material from the *Dreamfield* video comes from the Crescenti Moon Production, which debuted in 1994. Comments from Tim Crescenti are from our summer 2000 telephone interview. *The Baseball Encyclopedia* I consulted was the 1985 edition. Veda Ponikvar's "His Was a Life of Greatness" obituary of "Moonlight" Graham was published August 31, 1965, in the *Chisholm Free Press,* but I quoted it from a card published by the Doc Graham Memorial Scholarship Fund. For more information about the Doc "Moonlight" Graham Scholarship Fund and stories of "Moonlight" Graham, visit www.cardmall.com/monlight-graham. Al Ameskamp's comments were recorded during an interview conducted in person in summer 2000.

Chapter 3 Notes

Sources for this chapter include dialogue quoted from the marriage of Jerry Ryan and Lynn Burke that was part of the *Dreamfield* video (1994). Jerry and Lynn Ryan's comments come from a telephone interview and an e-mail dialogue conducted during summer 2000. Additional Ryan quotations come from *Dreamfield* (1994). Jerry Ryan's as-yet-unpublished poem was provided by the author. Quotations from *Field of Dreams* are taken directly from the 1998 DVD version of the film. Quotations from *Shoeless Joe* are taken directly from W. P. Kinsella's 1982 book. The comments from Iowa Film Office manager Wendol Jarvis come from an interview conducted in person during summer 2000. W. P. Kinsella's comments about Iowa are quoted from an August 15, 1989, *Philadelphia Inquirer* article titled "There's More to Kinsella's Literary Trove Than Baseball" and from his 1984 collection of short stories, *The Thrill of the Grass*. His comments about a perfect world come from an article titled "Baseball Like It Ought to Be," which appeared in the May 1989 edition of *American Film*. James Earl Jones's comments were recorded during a summer 2000 interview. Comments from the Field of Dreams tourist brochure are quoted from the Field of Dreams Movie Site's "Group Tour Information 2000." Comments from Tim Crescenti are from our summer 2000 telephone interview. Al Ameskamp's thoughts were recorded during an interview conducted in person in summer 2000. Camp Courageous associate executive director Mike Fortman's remarks come from a telephone interview conducted in fall 2000. Stacy Brannan's quotations come from various e-mails received during summer 2000. Thomas King's article about the Field of Dreams appeared in the *Wall Street Journal* on July 27, 1995. Tom O'Brien's review in *Commonweal* appeared on May 19, 1989. Marv Maiers's comments come from an interview conducted in person in fall 2000. Herb Caen's and Bowie Kuhn's quotations were picked from David Plaut's 1992 collection of baseball quotations titled *Baseball Wit and Wisdom*. Charles Fruehling Springwood's book *Cooperstown to Dyersville: A Geography of Baseball Nostalgia* was published in 1996.

Chapter 4 Notes

Sources for this chapter include comments from a telephone interview with Minister Terry Rush conducted during summer 2000. Additional material was quoted from the *Dreamfield* video (1994). Mircea Eliade's *The Sacred and the Profane* was published in 1957. Quotations from *Shoeless Joe* are taken directly from W. P. Kinsella's 1982 book. Wes Westrum's quotation was picked from a from David Plaut's 1992 collection of baseball quotations titled *Baseball Wit and Wisdom*. The song "Brother Noah Gave Out Checks for Rain" was written by Arthur Longbrake and copyrighted in 1907. A. Bartlett Giamatti's comments are quoted from the 1989 book *Take Time for Paradise*. The polling data about religious beliefs is taken from a survey conducted by Princeton Survey Research Associates, April 13–14, 2000, as reported by the University of Connecticut's Roper Center for Public Opinion Research.

Vinnie and Nancy Caruso's comments were taken from a series of telephone interviews conducted during fall 2000. Abraham Lincoln's Gettysburg Address is quoted from the Library of Congress's website, lcweb.loc.gov/exhibits/gadd. Vicky Maus's comments come from an interview conducted in person during fall 2000. Darrel Christenson's comments are taken from a telephone interview conducted in fall 2000.

Chapter 5 Notes

Sources for this chapter include comments from a telephone interview with Mark Babiarz conducted during fall 2000. Christopher Albrecht's comments were quoted from a fall 2000 telephone interview. Additional material from the Babiarz–Albrecht meeting were taken from Mark Babiarz's videotape of the event and a *Dubuque Telegraph Herald* account of the meeting. Bible quotations come straight from the good book. The Ronettes released the single "The (Best Part of) Breakin' Up" in 1964. Peaches and Herb's "Reunited" is from the 1979 album *Night Songs*. Paul Simon's "Mother and Child Reunion" is from the 1972 album *Paul Simon*. Quotations from *Shoeless Joe* are taken directly from W. P. Kinsella's 1982 book. Stephen Mosher's "Fielding Our Dreams: Rounding Third in Dyersville," was published in the eighth volume of the *Sociology of Sport Journal* in 1991. A. Bartlett Giamatti's comments are quoted from the 1989 book *Take Time for Paradise*. Phil Alden Robinson's comments were recorded during a telephone conversation in fall 2000. Quotations from *Field of Dreams* are taken directly from the 1998 DVD version of the film. Quotations from Carl Peterson and Phyllis Bethke come from a fall 2000 telephone interview.

Chapter 6 Notes

Sources for this chapter include comments from telephone interviews with Kent and John Nelson conducted during summer 2000. Additional material was quoted from the *Dreamfield* video (1994). Quotations from *Field of Dreams* are taken directly from the 1998 DVD version of the film. Ken Burns's comments are from the 1994 companion book to his film on baseball, *Baseball: An Illustrated History*. W.

P. Kinsella's comments about writing about baseball are quoted from
the 1998 *Field of Dreams* DVD. Quotations from *Shoeless Joe* are taken
directly from W. P. Kinsella's 1982 book. John P. Rossi's *The National
Game: Baseball and American Culture* was published in 2000. David
McGimpsey's *Imagining Baseball* also appeared in 2000. Roger Angell's
comments about the sugarcoating of baseball appeared in *The New
Yorker* (July 31, 1989). Phil Alden Robinson's comments were recorded
during a telephone conversation in fall 2000. His comment about
growing up as a baseball fan is from the May 1989 edition of *American
Film*. Donald Hall's comments on fathers and sons and catches come
from *Fathers Playing Catch with Sons: Essays on Sport (Mostly Baseball)*,
which was published in 1985. Bob Boone's comments were recorded
during a conversation in summer 2000. James Earl Jones's comments
were recorded during a summer 2000 telephone interview. Comments
from Tim Crescenti are from our summer 2000 telephone interview.
Vinnie Caruso's remarks are taken from a series of telephone interviews conducted during fall 2000. Ron Rosenbaum's "What *Is* It with
Guys and Baseball?" appeared in the July 1989 edition of *Mademoiselle*.
Ila Borders's comments come from a telephone interview conducted
during summer 2000. The information from the multimarket study
conducted by Major League Baseball in 2000 is taken from the official
Major League Baseball website, www.majorleaguebaseball.com. Doris
Kearns Goodwin's *Wait till Next Year: A Memoir* appeared in 1998.
Accounts of Haruyoshi Hori's ballfield come from Charles Fruehling
Springwood's "'America' in Takamiya: Transforming Japanese Rice
Paddies into Corn Stalks, Bleachers, and Basepaths," published in
Games, Sports, and Cultures (2000), a video of the Ghost Players' trip
to Japan, and an article titled "Baseball Dream Turns a Japanese Rice
Paddy into an Iowa Cornfield" that appeared September 13, 1995, in
the *Washington Post*. Keith Rahe's comments come from an interview conducted in person in fall 2000. Seigo Yamada's comments are
quoted from a fall 2000 interview. Takeshi Horie's comments come
from a fall 2000 interview.

Chapter 7 Notes

Sources for this chapter include my interview with Jim Bohn conducted by telephone in fall 2000. Quotations from *Field of Dreams* are taken directly from the 1998 DVD version of the film. W. P. Kinsella's comments about a perfect world come from an article titled "Baseball Like It Ought to Be," which appeared in the May 1989 edition of *American Film*. Phil Alden Robinson's comments were recorded during a telephone conversation in fall 2000 and taken from the 1998 *Field of Dreams* DVD. Jerry Ryan's as-yet-unpublished poem was provided by the author. Burt Lancaster's quotation is taken from the 1998 *Field of Dreams* DVD. The comment from the Dyersville visitors' guides comes from "Is This Heaven? . . . No, It's . . . Dyersville Farm Toy Capital of the World Visitors Guide." Mircea Eliade's *The Sacred and the Profane* was published in 1957. Nancy Caruso's comments were taken from a series of telephone interviews conducted during fall 2000. A. Bartlett Giamatti's comments are quoted from the 1989 book *Take Time for Paradise*. Robert D. Putnam's *Bowling Alone* was published in 2000. The account of Pat Buchanan's visit to the Field of Dreams comes from an article titled "Still They Come," which appeared in the *St. Petersburg Times* on October 21, 1995. Kent Nelson's comments are quoted from a telephone interview conducted during summer 2000. Al Vigil's remarks come from an interview conducted in person during fall 2000. Al and Rita Ameskamp's comments were recorded during an interview conducted in person in summer 2000. Bobby Fong's "The Magic Cocktail: The Enduring Appeal of the 'Field of Dreams'" was published in the fall 1993 edition of *Aethlon*. Brian Frankish's quotations were recorded during a fall 2000 telephone conversation. Timothy Busfield's comments are quoted from our fall 2000 telephone interview and from the 1998 *Field of Dreams* DVD. The words of Langston Hughes come from his poem "Montage of a Dream Deferred." The material about the Acres of Diamonds speech and Russell Conwell come from the Temple University website, www.temple.edu/about/temples_founder.html.

Index

About the Author

Brett H. Mandel is a writer and consultant in Philadelphia where he is engaged in civic activism and government reform efforts. Previously, Brett served as the executive director of the National Education Technology Funding Corporation, a private, nonprofit organization that worked to help local public school districts access cost-effective financing for school construction and renovation. Brett also served as executive director of Philadelphia Forward, a citizens' organization promoting tax, government, and ethics reform; and as director of financial and policy analysis in the City of Philadelphia Office of the Controller. Brett received his undergraduate degree from Hamilton College and his graduate degree in governmental administration from the University of Pennsylvania.

Brett is the primary author of *Philadelphia: A New Urban Direction* (Saint Joseph's University Press, 1999), a vision of Philadelphia's likely future without change and a comprehensive plan designed to make Philadelphia a preferred place to live, work, and visit. The book received the National Association of Local Government Auditors Special Project Award. Another book, *Minor Players, Major Dreams* (University of Nebraska Press, 1997), written from his perspective as an author signed to a Minor League Baseball player's contract, tells the inside story of Minor League life. His next book, *Philadelphia: Corrupt and*

Consented, about the city's struggle with municipal corruption, is due to be published in 2021.

A lifelong Philadelphian, Brett is the commissioner of the Greater Philadelphia Men's Adult Baseball League and the board chair of the Circadium: School of Contemporary Circus, America's first school of higher education for circus arts. Brett lives in the Fitler Square neighborhood of Philadelphia with his wife and three children.

CPSIA information can be obtained
at www.ICGtesting.com
Printed in the USA
BVHW032012091020
590732BV00002B/3

9 781493 055104